Waterside Wirral

Photography by
Guy Huntington

The Bluecoat Press

Canada Geese

Waterside Wirral
First published in Great Britain by
The Bluecoat Press, Liverpool 1998

All photographs by
Guy Huntington

Book design & typesetting by
March Design, Liverpool

Printed by
GZ Printek

All rights reserved. No part of this publication may be reproduced or transmitted in any form or by any means, electronic or mechanical, including photocopying, recording or any information storage and retrieval system without prior permission in writing from the publisher.

ISBN 1 872568 44 0

Waterside Wirral

Foreword

Waterside Wirral is the first in a series of books about rivers in the Mersey Basin. The concept was devised jointly by staff of the Mersey Basin Trust and the Ramblers Association. The Ramblers work to protect footpaths and campaign vigorously for more freedom of access to mountain, moorland and other open country. They defend the beauty and diversity of Britain's countryside and have been lobbying successfully at national and local levels for sixty years. They can be contacted at:

> The Ramblers Association
> 1/5 Wandsworth Road
> London SWG 2XX
> Telephone 0171 339 8500

This book has been produced by staff of the Mersey Basin Trust and members of RiVa 2005 river valley initiative working with Bluecoat Press – an undertaking which reflects the partnership approach of the Mersey Basin Campaign.

Members of the river valley initiative gave their time and specialist knowledge, motivated by their wish to see the aims of the Mersey Basin Campaign realised in the improvement and celebration of Wirral's watercourses.

One of the aims of RiVa 2005 is to improve access to Wirral's rivers and streams, where appropriate, so that they can be appreciated by as many people as possible. This book uniquely focuses on routes for walkers, cyclists and horse riders along rivers, streams and river valleys. We hope people will use it to explore the Wirral and to discover the varied interests of its watersides. Please respect the environment in which you find yourself, whether it is urban or rural, and help us in this way to protect and enhance our natural assets.

RiVa 2005 is indebted to Clare O'Sullivan who compiled this book. Thanks also go to the contributors – Hilary Ash, Penny Becket and members of RiVa 2005 Access Working Group, in particular representitives of Groundwork, Wirral, Metropolitan Borough of Wirral and Wirral Footpaths & Open Spaces Society, together with the RiVa 2005 co-ordinator. Partners in RiVa 2005 have also provided financial assistance for the production of this book.

Cowslips

The Mersey Basin Campaign

The Mersey Basin Campaign is the 25-year Government-backed partnership which brings together local authorities, businesses, voluntary organisations and government-sponsored agencies to deliver water quality improvements and waterside regeneration throughout the Mersey Basin river system.

The Campaign covers High Peak in Derbyshire, Greater Manchester, Cheshire, Merseyside and south Lancashire – an area of around 4,680 square kilometres with 2,000 kilometres of watercourses.

The aims of the Campaign, which was launched in 1985, are:
- to improve water quality so that all rivers, streams and canals are clean enough to support fish
- to stimulate the development of attractive waterside environments for businesses, housing, tourism, heritage, recreation and wildlife
- to encourage people to value and cherish their watercourses and waterfront environments

At its core, the Mersey Basin Campaign has three organisations which aim to support the Campaign partnership, nurturing projects which contribute towards the Campaign's objectives.

The Mersey Basin Trust is a charity which encourages and supports action by volunteers, community organisations and schools through a variety of projects and grants schemes. It is estimated that since the launch of the Mersey Basin Campaign, the voluntary sector has contributed more than £1million in volunteers work alone (valued at £5 an hour) on waterside improvements and activities, in addition to attracting funding from businesses and grants schemes into the region.

The Mersey Basin Business Foundation acts as a channel for business resources to support the Campaign. It provides all its members with a forum within the Campaign and has attracted well over £1million in funding from Campaign partners

The Mersey Basin Campaign Administration Ltd. is grant-aided by the Government to promote, manage and support the Campaign effort; implementing and facilitating policy and action.

River valley initiatives are local partnerships which focus the aims of the Mersey Basin Campaign on specific river valleys within the Campaign area. These partnerships include local authorities, businesses, voluntary and community organisations. They are supported by the central Campaign organisations, but set their own agendas in response to local needs and opportunities within the framework of the Campaign's objectives.

The Mersey Basin Campaign
Sunley Tower
Piccadilly Plaza
Manchester M1 4BE
Telephone 0161 952 4279

RiVa 2005

RiVa 2005 is the Mersey Basin Campaign's River valley initiative for the Wirral Peninsula. It is committed to promoting and protecting Wirral's rivers and streams. The name RiVa 2005 is taken from 'River Valley Action', 2005 is the year by which the main objective of the initiative, along with subsidiary ones is to be met. The main objective is to bring all of Wirral's watercourses up to the standard where they can support fish life.

All the rivers and streams flow north and east across the Wirral peninsula before reaching the Mersey estuary. They run through rural countryside, nature reserves, villages, towns and industrial areas. This means that they and the land surrounding them can be susceptible to pollution from either domestic or industrial sources.

Hence, there is a stark contrast as to the most effective methods of improving the quality of both land and water in the various areas.

There are many stretches of Wirral's river systems which would be improved by such activities as rubbish clearance, bank maintenance, footpath laying and tree or wildflower planting.

This is where RiVa 2005 comes into its own. It can assist with placing willing volunteers into environmentally aware groups, or there may be groups which need assistance with funding, arranging or organising projects. Maybe you are already part of a group which uses or carries out improvements on a Wirral watercourse, if so RiVa 200S can help you get the most from your project.

RiVa 2005 is constantly working to increase awareness and appreciation of Wirral's rivers and streams, improve access to them, encourage local community participation in their protection and enhance their value for nature conservation.

This publication is one element of the campaign which we hope will help to encourage Wirral residents and visitors to the area discover the often hidden asset which are its watercourses.

RiVa 2005
Ivy Farm
Arrowe Country Park
Arrowe Park Road
Upton
Wirral L49 5LW
Telephone 0151 677 2439

DON'T FORGET

1 Always keep to designated paths
This is to avoid environmental damage and also for your own safety.

2 Public footpaths are for walkers only. Horses and cycles are prohibited.

3 Bridleways are for people on horseback or on foot. Pedal cycles are allowed, but they must give way to horses. Working lights must be used after dark.

4 Do not go near ponds or rivers alone.

5 Help to keep all water clean. Never drop litter, not only does it look unsightly but it is hazardous to wildlife.

6 Protect wildlife – Do not pick any flowers, as some species are rare or only grow in localised patches.

7 Fasten all gates after use.

8 Guard against fire – Even a discarded cigarette may be enough to start a fire.

9 Make sure that dogs are kept under guard.

Peacock

Waterfall,
Thornton Stream

Wirral's rivers and streams

Ask about Wirral's rivers and many, if not most people, will respond with surprise: 'Rivers? ... are there any rivers on the Wirral?'.

The River Dee and the River Mersey are familiar enough. Their tidal estuaries define Wirral's coastline. But inland rivers? Surely not that drainage ditch at the end of the garden? Or that flood channel glimpsed from a moving train?

The problem of recognition lies within our own imagination and experience. We think of rivers as wide and deep. The waters sparkle in the sun and flow on for many miles. Rivers can be used to fish in, boat on or even just sit beside. Thought of in those terms, such inland rivers do not exist on the Wirral.

But there are rivers. Only small rivers, perhaps, but rivers which, in the past, influenced the form and nature of Wirral's landscape and which, in the present day, continue to form an important part of the natural scene. They flow through a variety of landscapes from open fields and small wooded valleys to built up areas and flat, marshy land. Sometimes these streams are valued as part of a wider landscape, but more often they are sadly abused, used as a means of carrying away dirty water, for flytipping or simply disregarded altogether.

How many of us notice when we cross by road over the course of a stream? Do we ever wonder why the road at that point can often dip down into a hollow and then up again? Do we ask ourselves why some of Wirral's established woodland is often to be found growing close to streams, or even consider just why our housing estate has such an uneven boundary? There may, of course, be several reasons why such features occur. Not least among these is our own manipulation of the landscape for flood protection or land-use purposes. But, because Wirral's rivers are so small and, in relative terms insignificant, we tend not to notice them at all as we go about our daily lives.

This book attempts to redress the balance by promoting Wirral's rivers and streams as an important but forgotten part of Wirral's natural heritage.

This section attempts a more general, selective account which puts into context the information that follows. It presupposes that the more we can learn about the small rivers and streams that meander through the Wirral, the more likely we are to value the natural environment of which we are all an integral part.

Clatter Brook running through Thornton Wood

The Mersey and Dee Basins

Marsh marigolds at Clatter Brook, Thornton Wood

The primary watershed of the Wirral is that between the Mersey Basin and the Dee Basin. It runs roughly parallel to the north/south route of the A540. Within the Mersey Basin, there are a number of secondary catchment areas, two of which are described in more detail later in this section.

The streams of the Dee catchment area are mostly rivulets which trickle to the estuary mud and sand; firstly through exposed sandstone gullies and then through the clay cliffs. Two of these streams, Shotwick Brook, and an unnamed stream that cuts down through the area known as the Dungeon are worthy of note for their particular conservation and landscape value.

The larger of Wirral's two drainage basins, the Mersey Basin, contains the principle inland rivers of the Wirral and sub-divides into two secondary catchment areas, namely the Birket Catchment (Wallasey Pool) and the Dibbin Catchment (Bromborough Pool). The Birket catchment area ($62km^2$) drains the northern part of the Wirral by the River Birket and its tributaries. The Dibbin catchment area ($65km^2$) drains the more central section of the Wirral via the River Dibbin and its associated streams, which include the Clatter Brook and Thornton Brook.

Snowdrops at Clatter Brook, Thornton Wood

The Birket catchment
The Wallasey Pool

Wild flower meadow at Meols near the River Birket

The River Birket

The Birket is a designated main river maintained for flood control purposes. Without such flood prevention measures, which include the construction of a sea wall along the North Wirral coast, pumping stations and raised earthbunds along the Birket and the Fender, most of the low-lying land of the North Wirral Plain would be under water during tidal surges.

Since the need for such flood control is paramount, the Birket is heavily engineered and visually dull as it cuts through an often bleak, windswept landscape. Little vegetation is permitted to grow on its banks and its channel has been deepened and straightened to increase its water-holding capacity. Yet the open land (such as the area known as Meols Meadows) through which it passes yields up some occasional surprises: reed beds and ponds fringed with trees and shrubs or hay meadows which sustain lapwings, skylarks and rare flowers.

Arrowe Park Lake. The River Birket has been dammed here to create a small ornamental lake

The Tributaries of the River Birket: The Fender, Arrowe Brook and Newton Brook

The Fender is one of three tributaries that feed directly into the River Birket. The other two tributaries are the Arrowe Brook (itself joined by Greasby Brook) and Newton Brook. The Fender, like the Birket, is also subject to flood control measures and for much of its length is no more than a drainage ditch. It flows south to north towards the Birket between two prominent ridges of exposed sandstone. Indeed, the Fender valley is the largest and widest of all the river valleys on the Wirral, effectively separating the western side of the Wirral from that of the east. Unfortunately, the Fender river itself is for the most part an insignificant channel, often hidden from view though not underground, along its own valley floor. Much of the reason for this is that the Fender must compete for space in a corridor of land which contains a motorway (the M53), an industrial estate, railway lines, pylons, sewers and all the other paraphernalia that are accompaniments to modern urban living.

Only for a short length near its source at Storeton does the Fender retain something of its former rural character. In its unregarded, unnoticed state the Fender, for much of its length, is a rather

Bidston Moss. Since 1994, the area has been a designated Local Nature Reserve. Ponds, paths and boardwalks have been constructed to enable limited access to a site rich in wildlife

sad river which deserves more attention and care than it presently enjoys.

In contrast, its own tributary, Prenton Brook, is a delightful natural stream which flows through open fields and a long wooded valley between Thingwall and Barnston. At Barnston Dale, the setting for the brook is lovely and is easily equal, in landscape terms at least, to anything that can be found on the Wirral.

The Arrowe Brook is the second main tributary of the Birket. It appears to have maintained its natural course without too much alteration. Where such change is evident, it is mostly close to urban development (usually housing estates) built up to its edge. The only major exception to this is when the stream enters Arrowe Park. It seems possible that sometime in the past the stream was diverted from Limbo Lane (Irby) into the Park to join up two sub-catchments. The waterfall is probably due to the differences in level exposed at the Arrowe Park end. Further into the Park, the stream has been dammed to create a small lake, a high, ornamental weir and, further downstream, shallow, stepped weirs.

The Arrowe Brook rises at Pensby and joins the Birket between Meols and Leasowe. Along its course, it passes through a variety of landscapes, from the rather bitty, urban fringe land at Pensby, alongside a housing estate to the low-lying North Wirral Plain. At Irby, it passes through the wooded valley of Harrock Wood, an attractive mixed woodland owned by the National Trust. Then alongside housing at Limbo Lane Plantation, across to and through Arrowe Park and on to skirt the side of Upton Meadow beyond. North of Greasby Road, it runs alongside more housing before briefly entering open fields at Saughall Massie. The Arrowe Brook then turns abruptly through and alongside more urban development on its way to the Birket.

The layouts of the areas of housing built alongside the Arrowe Brook rarely, it seems, acknowledge the stream as a visual asset. Garden fences screen the Arrowe Brook from the people who live next to it. The Brook, in common with other streams on the Wirral where development runs alongside, is seen too often in negative terms: as a physical limit to development, as a drainage ditch necessary to remove surface water, as a dumping-ground for garden rubbish ('out of sight, out of mind') and as an easy route to build sewers alongside.

The potential of these streams seems rarely explored by those who live alongside them. And yet the streams are rich in small detail and provide a natural corridor of real value. Where footpaths run alongside the Arrowe Brook this potential can easily be seen in the small, muddy oxbows left by the straightening of the channel, in the gentle meanders around mature trees, in the edge fringed with waterside vegetation, such as willows and alders, that garden birds enjoy for shelter and food. Even the bed of the stream is of interest. Sometimes the channel is deep cut through the boulder clay, sometimes sandstone outcrops are revealed in the side of the bank or sandstone is cut away on the channel bed. Always the water continues to move, slowly but inevitably, towards the sea.

Further to the west, Greasby Brook links with the Arrowe Brook at Saughall Massie, having first skirted around the edge of the urban areas of Irby and Greasby. It is shorter than the Arrowe Brook and, for over half its length, its course is through countryside. It begins in farmland close to the Thurstaston Road as a shallow meandering stream and soon enters the mixed woodland of Thurstaston Common and, as with Harrock Wood, this is National Trust owned land which is open to the public. It makes its way across the common on its eastern edge past Royden Park to the hollow on Hillbark Road. From there, it passes across open land, then alongside housing, all the time fringed with overgrown hedgerows and willows. North of Frankby Road, this vegetation, particularly the willows, have

Pond beside the Birket, Leasowe

been badly damaged by the storms of 1990 and the stream displays the now familiar signs of misuse. Beyond Greasby, the stream is linked by a perimeter drain to Newton Brook before it meets the Arrowe Brook, in open fields again.

Newton Brook is the third and shortest of the main tributaries of the Birket river. No more than a small stream, it rises below Stapledon Wood between Caldy and West Kirby and marks the garden boundaries of housing between Column Road and Newton. In doing so, it turns sharply to the west to China Farm Lane at Larton. Here the stream has cut a two metre deep channel revealing sandstone in the stream bed. It has little associated vegetation beside it. The Brook again skirts the boundary of a relatively new housing development and then heads northwards towards Newton Bridge on the Saughall Massie Road, passing first between some fields of unimproved grassland and later farmed pasture edged by low hedgerows. Beyond Newton Bridge, it follows a natural course before joining the Birket close to Fornall's Green at Meols. From this point onwards, the Birket is easily identifiable as a flood controlled river and is heavily engineered. At Fornall's Green Lane, it has been put into a deep, concrete channel, fenced to prevent access and, as it heads east near Meols Station, is screened from view behind a low clipped hedge. Around this area, too, is evidence of the Birket's flood potential, with earth embankments built around the edge of housing acting as dams against any such flood.

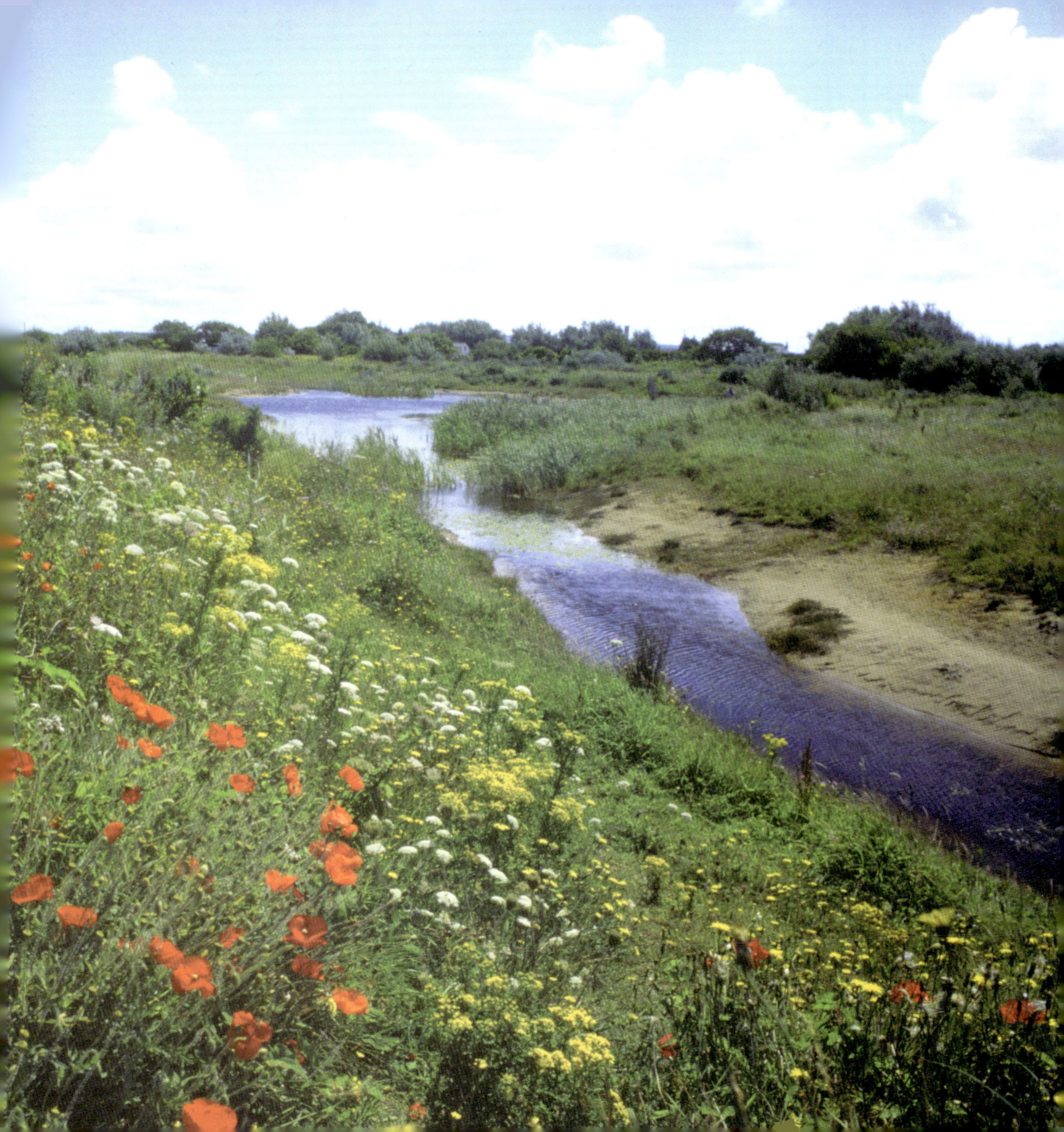

Thornton Wood,
Clatter Brook

The Dee estuary has been silting up since Roman times but the process has been accelerated this century with the introduction of cord-grass

Thurstaston Common high up on a sandstone ridge overlooking the River Dee

Wirral's natural history: the life around you

Two hundred million years ago, long before mankind existed to take note, a large river was emptying its load of sand in a flat delta between what we now call the Pennines and the Welsh mountains. Over millennia, that sand formed the red Triassic sandstone familiar to Wirral residents. Earth movements broke and tilted the rocks; a small but clear example of the resulting 'faults' can be seen at Mill Road, Bromborough. The land was formed into two parallel ridges, running north-west to south-east. The higher western one forms the hills of Thurstaston, Grange and Caldy, crowned by heathland, and extends through Heswall to Burton. The eastern one is lower and more broken, stretching from New Brighton and Wallasey through Bidston to Storeton.

The Ice Ages came and went over northern Europe. When the last ice sheets melted ten thousand years ago, they left boulder clay, pebbles and sand spread over all the land between and around the sandstone ridges. Some of that clay, at New Ferry, Meols and Eastham, has been extensively dug for bricks. New Ferry sewage works sits within a former claypit, alongside the wartime Pluto tank. Around them grow reedbeds where reed- and sedge-warblers breed, and a large colony of an uncommon dwarf broom called dyer's greenweed (used to dye wool yellow).

The clay is also responsible for one of Wirral's most notable wildlife features, our ponds. The surface soils of the area tend to be acid, which makes them poor for our main crop plants. However, some 2-3m down there is a layer of chalky boulder clay called marl. Farmers from Roman times dug this up to spread on the fields to sweeten the soil. The practice was most popular in the 17th century and died out as lime became available with the advent of canals and railways. Dig holes in clay and sooner of later most fill with water. Consequently, north-west England has the greatest density of ponds in Europe; between them they are home to a large variety of plants and animals. Plants grow in the water (like pondweeds and water lilies), in the shallows (reedmace, bur-reed, reed) and on the moist edges (yellow flag, loosestrife, brooklime, bogbean and many more). This variety of plants, different in each pond, supports many invertebrates – beetles, dragonflies, boatmen, skaters and all the 'mini-beasts' which are such fun to find on pond-dips. On these feed various birds and amphibians – frogs, toads and newts, including in many Wirral ponds, the rare and decreasing great crested or warty newt. This species has become so rare across Europe that it is legally protected. It is a handsome animal, up to 12cm long and with a black and orange patterned underside. Only the male has a crest. They do sometimes use garden ponds, and more frequently feed and hibernate in gardens, where they are useful controllers of slugs! If you think you have them, do not disturb or handle. English Nature or Cheshire Wildlife Trust can give advice.

Geological processes have not stood still since the last Ice Age. Coastal erosion and deposition have reshaped the coastline and continue to do so. At the north end of Wirral the land once extended considerably further than at present. From Victorian times until the 1980s, the stumps of a wood could be seen on the shore at Meols. The erosion would be continuing but for the embankment erected in the 1970s, which also protects the plain

Great crested newt, now a rare and protected species still found in many Wirral ponds

behind from flooding. The embankment removed large stretches of sand dunes, and our best ones are now between West Kirby and Red Rocks, and inside golf courses, with a small area at Leasowe gunsite. Sand dunes are tough habitats; dry, hot, salty and storm-prone, requiring special adaptations in the plants that live there. Several grasses especially marram help build the dunes. As sand blown from the shore accumulates around their stems they grow up through it, collecting more. In time the dunes stabilise, and smaller flowers move in, such as wild thyme, kidney vetch and clovers. In the damp areas between rows of dunes (slacks) creeping willow and, at Red Rocks, a rare horsetail can be found. These more sheltered areas are home to many insects and can be buzzing with bees, grasshoppers and butterflies on a summer's day. At Red Rocks the pools also support a small population of the very rare Natterjack Toad. Red Rocks has changed considerably since West Kirby marine lake was enlarged a decade ago, and has become less suitable for the toads. English Nature and Cheshire Wildlife Trust (who manage the area as a reserve) are trying to re-vitalise the population with spawn from Ainsdale, artificial ponds and fencing. A new line of dunes is building, and these should eventually provide a new slack area for the toads and marsh plants. The reserve is always open, but please keep to the paths.

Erosion is also gradually attacking the clay cliffs along the Dee between Heswall and West Kirby. Those at Thurstaston are a Site of Special Scientific Interest (SSSI) because of the variety of minerals in them, and the unusual plants which grow along them. These include small short-lived plants, such as centaury and yellow-wort, for whom the continued erosion is vital, to prevent denser vegetation from smothering them.

Coastal deposition has changed the Dee estuary within living memory. The estuary has been silting up since Roman times, driving the port steadily downstream from Burton via Neston, Parkgate, Gayton and Dawpool to Hoylake. The process has accelerated since the Dee was canalised to the Welsh side in the 19th century, helped by the unfortunate introduction of cord-grass. The extensive marshes may not be attractive to everyone, but they are vital to many tens of thousands of birds. Both our estuaries are internationally important over-wintering areas for huge flocks of wildfowl and waders, such as dunlin, knot, oystercatchers, redshank, turnstone, curlew and purple sandpiper. Most of these birds migrate to northern breeding grounds in summer. As the tide rises, the birds move inshore or onto coastal fields to roost, flying in great flocks which wheel and turn in spectacular fashion. Do not disturb the roosting birds; they use up valuable energy in avoiding you. The RSPB and Ranger Service run regular bird-watches, especially when high tides bring the birds close. Both the Dee and the Mersey now have strategies drawn up to try to conserve them and to avoid conflict between different human uses. The Mersey is getting steadily cleaner as the Mersey Basin Campaign takes effect, and fish are returning. In the longer term change is inevitable, both natural and the man-made change of rising sea levels caused by global warming. This rise will reduce the marsh areas, and the birds may fare badly unless we are prepared to allow reclaimed areas to revert to marsh.

Mankind came to Wirral in Stone Age times, and since then has steadily reshaped our landscape. Celtic residents gave us names such as Landican and Liscard. The Romans had a road through the peninsula and an extensive settlement at Meols, now washed away. The Anglo-Saxons arrived in the 7th century (Willaston, Eastham, Sutton) and the Vikings in the 9th (West Kirby, Frankby, Irby and their parliament site at Thingwall). By Domesday, Wirral was more densely populated than most of England – but at only 405 recorded families, the total was probably no more than 2000! Very little woodland is recorded, at Mollington, Tranmere and Prenton. The narrow woods fringing the

*Knot flying over Hilbre
Island in the Dee Estuary*

Southern hawker, just clinging to its larval skin

Dibbin and Rivacre Brook, plus some other smaller pieces, must have been overlooked, as they show every sign of being ancient woodlands. From late Norman times until 1376, Wirral was a Royal Forest. 'Forest' did not imply woodland in those days, merely that the peasants had to live with even more restrictions than usual, to the advantage of the king and court who wanted a ready supply of game for winter food. Much of Wirral at the time must have been heath, scrub and some woodland, with relatively little cultivated land.

Nowadays woodland covers about 3% of Wirral, well below the national average. Ancient woodland, generally the most valuable for wildlife and attractive to people, accounts for under half of that. However we are fortunate to have long stretches at Dibbinsdale (an SSSI) and Rivacre (Site of Biological Importance), both of which are Country Parks. Neither brook supports much life; they are shaded by trees and have poor water quality, dropping to the lowest pollution classification at times in the lower Dibbin. Both also suffer from 'scour' – the sudden rush of water when rain runs rapidly from built areas, sweeping aquatic life downstream. However their steep banks have ensured the survival of some of the most attractive places in Wirral. Take a walk in April from Bromborough Rake Station, when the wood anemones star the floor with white. And another in May when the bluebells are so dense the air is full of their scent. Ransoms flowers on damp areas at the Marfords, golden saxifrage curtains the rocks at Brotherton Park and the tiny moschatel, or town hall clock, is abundant at the lower end of Rivacre. Elsewhere, pignut is particularly abundant at Harrocks Wood near Irby, cuckoo pint at Upton Bridge Wood, Greasby and the woods of the Dungeon, near Heswall, hide Wirral's biggest waterfall.

The little stream flowing through the Dungeon is one of the few to drain to the Dee estuary. It has good water quality, and a rare caddis fly has been found there. The only other sizable stream to enter the Dee is Shotwick Brook, at the very south of the peninsula. There are areas of old wood and grassland along this, but they are private land. Our woods are not only valuable for their flowers, although massed bluebells are a British speciality, almost unknown on the Continent. Many birds breed in them, including all three species of woodpecker, which rely on dead wood, especially standing dead trees. Large numbers of warblers, tits, thrushes and other small species spend at least part of the year in the woods, and migrants such as fieldfares and

Water beetle. Improvement to the water quality is being reflected in the variety of pond life being recorded

The pools at Red Rocks support a small population of the now rare natterjack toad

13

Badgers are a legally protected resident of the Wirral and are often associated with woodland, although they feed in a variety of places including heathland, farmland and sometimes lawns

redwings visit in winter. Bats are also closely associated with woods, especially where there is water. All our British bats are insect-eaters, and have declined so badly in the last 50 years that they are legally protected. So if you are honoured by bats in your attic, as I am, ask advice from Merseyside & Cheshire Bat Group. The Group will also be delighted to show you that bats are not the horrific creatures of fable, but attractive small furry creatures with amazing flying powers who do us a great favour by eating thousands of midges a night!

Another legally protected resident, the badger, is also often associated with woodland, although they feed in a variety of places including heathland, farmland and sometimes lawns. The cruel and illegal practice of badger digging is still a problem in this area, so sett locations are kept as secret as possible and monitored by Wirral & Cheshire Badger Group. Unfortunately with the spread of housing over the last century, some setts are now in the big gardens of Victorian houses, and we have regular problems with developers who want to build luxury dwellings for people and deprive poor old Brock of what little living space he has left.

Wirral's other main river system, the Birket and its tributaries, is in complete contrast to the Dibbin. The catchment is almost flat, and distinct valleys only occur in the upper reaches, such as Prenton Dell. There is little woodland, and even the actual course of the rivers has been considerably altered in the last century, to improve drainage of the flat landscape. The Environment Agency is just finishing another major flood relief scheme on the Birket and Fender. However the water quality is generally good, and there is far more aquatic life than in the Dibbin. Flowering rush decorates the banks of the Birket with its pink umbrellas in July, along with swathes of great yellow cress, and masses of pondweed provide for invertebrates. In places the tall grey clubrush occurs, a plant which usually frequents brackish habitats. Before Wallasey Pool was turned into docks about 1845, all of Bidston Marsh was regularly flooded on high tides. Now the various tippings have left almost no natural marshland, although a small Local Nature Reserve has been established near Bidston Station on tipped land. Somehow the grey clubrush survives. Golfers at Bidston might like to note the Old Courses which surround their land, where stonewort, an uncommon alga, thrives. At least, it does until the road drainage from Bidston bypass enters the flow, with its salt, rubber and oil, and ruins the water quality so that the stretch past the clubhouse is depressing.

Farming has re-shaped Wirral's landscape over the centuries and, as in much of England, the intensive agriculture of the last few decades has severely reduced our 'common' wildlife. Skylarks have lost half their population in that time because of changed farming methods. However, on the bank of the Arrowe Brook at Meols there survives a remnant of the 'old' English countryside, a small group of traditional haymeadows, the best on Merseyside and an SSSI. Such landscapes have declined by 99% in Cheshire since the 1940s. The small damp fields are a tapestry of wild flowers, including species now rare such as hay-rattle and pepper-saxifrage. Chimney-sweeper moths feed on the pignut, which lives in old grassland as well as old woods, and skylarks and lapwings breed. Unfortunately this little gem cannot be open to the public as it has to be farmed in the traditional manner, with a summer haycut and autumn grazing.

Building as much as agricultural change has been responsible for losses of another old agricultural landscape, our heathlands. These would once have stretched along both sandstone ridges but much of the eastern ridge has been built on, along with large areas at Heswall. Internationally, Western Europe has lost nearly all of its lowland heaths, making our British examples very special remnants. Most heathlands are a product of people grazing their animals over centuries on thin, poor, acid soils. Under such conditions, grasses

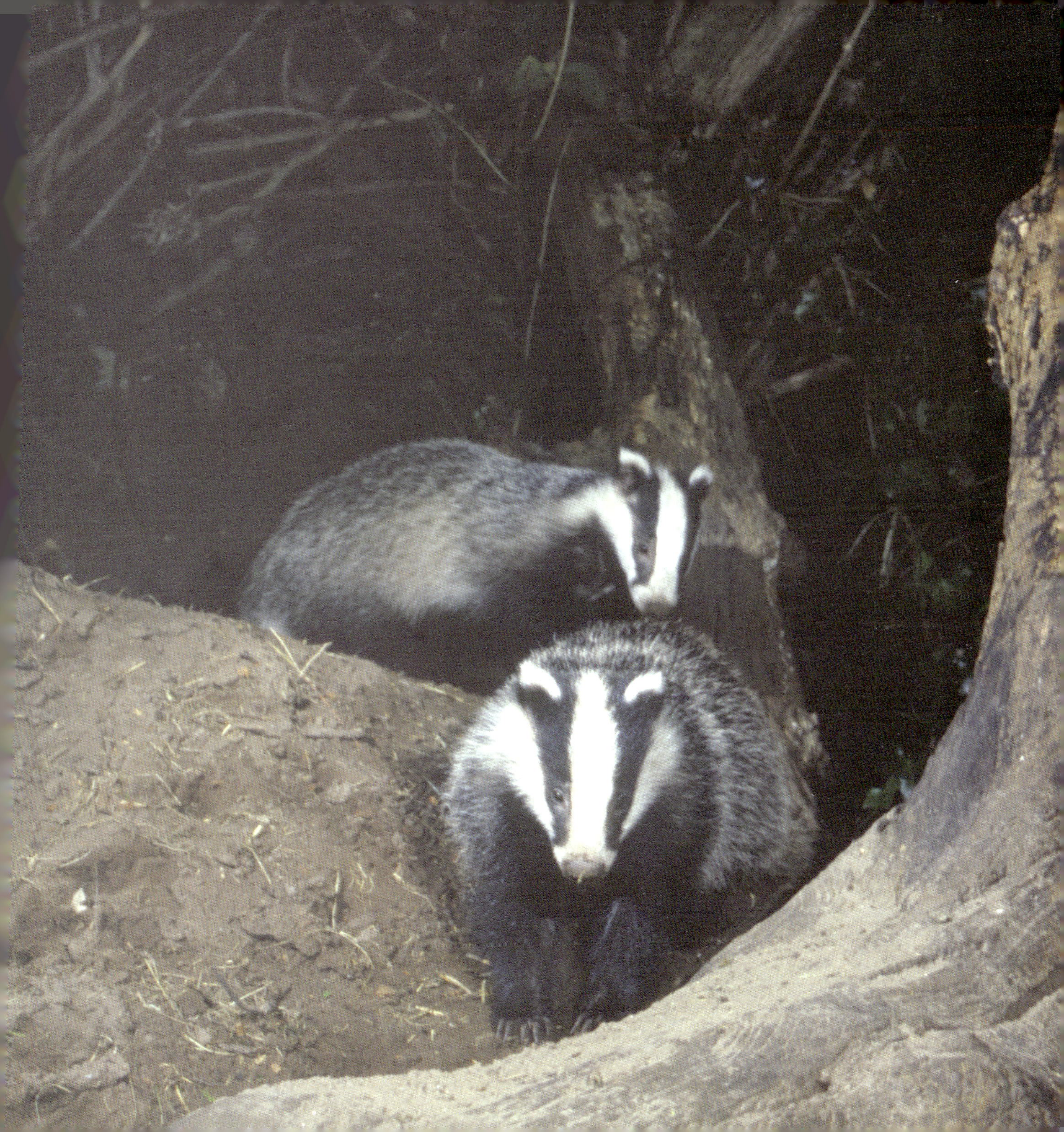

At New Ferry, the former railway goods yard, is now a butterfly park, capitalising on the natural colonisation of many butterflies, including the comma shown opposite, and other species to make a valuable educational site in a very dense urban area

and trees are replaced by dwarf shrubs: heather, bell heather, bilberry, cross-leaved heath and western gorse. The latter is a speciality of western Britain and flowers at the same time as the heather in August-September, giving spectacular displays of purple and yellow across Thurstaston Common. Certain insects depend on heathland conditions and, at Thurstaston, the silver-studded blue butterfly has recently been introduced from a threatened site in Shropshire. Local volunteers with Butterfly Conservation prepared the habitat for it, and early results are promising. The heathlands at Thurstaston and Heswall Dales also support lizards, though it is difficult to see these fast-moving and shy creatures. It is 20 years since the whirring call of the nightjar was heard on Thurstaston. The reason is natural change: as the grazing of the heaths has lapsed in the last half-century, so trees have started to grow again. Some areas, like Heswall Beacons and Irby Common, are now effectively woods, but woods with few species living in them and less value to wildlife in general than the heaths they replaced. The Ranger Service, with Countryside Stewardship money and a lot of volunteer help, has cleared much scrub over the last few years, and, on Thurstaston, the National Trust have re-introduced grazing, with a small flock of Herdwick sheep. Do go and see them, but keep any dogs under close control.

Wirral has changed greatly in the last 200 years. In the early 19th century, as Liverpool grew and steam ferries were developed, the cleaner air and attractive landscapes of Wirral became desirable residential areas. Birkenhead was developed with grandiose ideas, fuelled by new industry, especially shipbuilding. In 1810 it had 109 inhabitants. By 1841, there were 8000 and rising fast. Development spread along the new railway lines to Chester (built 1840) and Hoylake (completed 1866), and eventually to the salubrious air of Heswall. The process has continued since, helped by the railway tunnel (1886) and road tunnels (1936 & 1972), until large parts of northern Wirral have turned into suburbia. It has not been all loss to wildlife however. In some places, like Dibbinsdale and Heswall Dales, wildlife areas have been preserved among the building. In others, wildlife has moved back in as people have moved on. At New Ferry, the former railway goods yard is now a butterfly park, capitalising on the natural colonisation of many butterflies and other species to make a valuable educational site in a very dense urban area. The Park is the vision of local resident Mel Roberts, who campaigned for years to get it recognition and protection. Eventually British Rail granted a lease to Cheshire Wildlife Trust, who guide the local group which runs it. After 30 years of neglect and abuse, volunteers have put in huge amounts of work to clear rubbish, install paths, make a pond and manage the plantlife. Twenty-three species of butterfly have been seen, of which about 12 breed each year, along with many other 'mini-beasts', birds and amphibians. School groups need to book (contact below), but the Park is open Sunday afternoons May-August, next door to Bebington Station.

There are so many other places to talk about – Hilbre Islands, Storeton Woods, Eastham Country Park, Wirral Way.

Wirral has a remarkable amount of wildlife for its size. There are 11 SSSIs and over 70 Sites of Biological Importance in the peninsula, with a good proportion open to the public in Country Parks, the coastline and elsewhere. Do explore and value your wildlife – and help us to protect it for future generations!

Hilary J. Ash
Hon. Recording Officer, Wirral Wildlife.

Wirral Wildlife is the local group of Cheshire Wildlife Trust and is concerned with all wildlife in our area, working closely with the various specialist societies. Contacts for all organisations mentioned can be found via the Ranger Service or Liverpool Museum.
For New Ferry Butterfly Park, telephone Mel Roberts 0151 645 4849

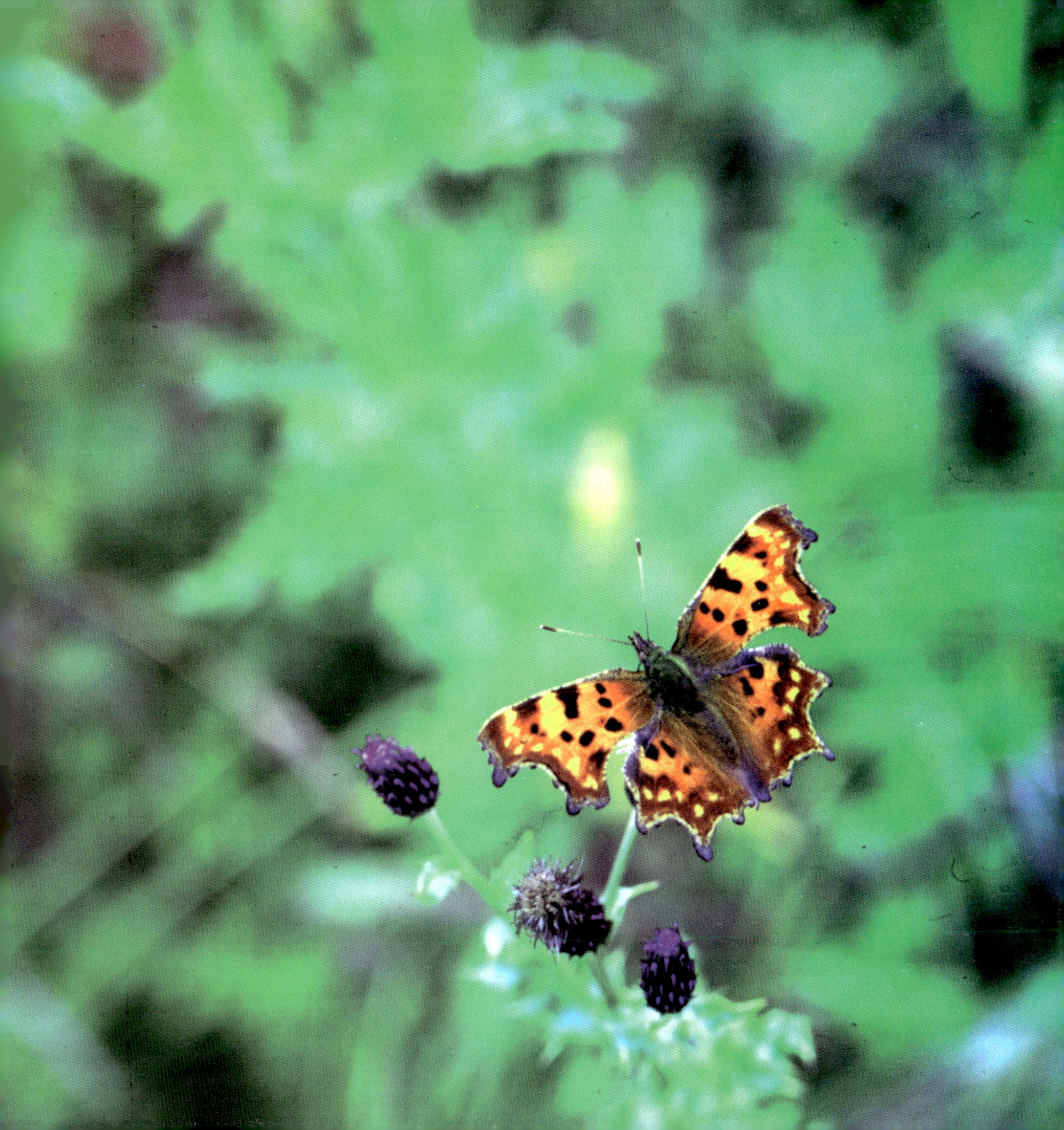

Meadow Brown

Common Blue

Tortoiseshell

The Dibbinsdale catchment
Bromborough Pool system

The River Dibbin and its tributaries

The Dibbin valley contains areas of high conservation and landscape value and, for much of its length, it is protected by statutory and other designations. At Dibbinsdale and Brotherton Park in Bromborough, for example, an area of 475 hectares was designated by the local authority as a Local Nature Reserve (LNR) in 1983. The river is also one of the best known on the Wirral, though it is more often referred to as the Dibbin Brook, a more fitting description, perhaps, than that of 'river'.

The Dibbin rises on rural land around the village of Ledsham in Cheshire but the source of its main tributary, the Clatter Brook, is to the north, close to Storeton and only a short distance from the River Fender's source in the Birket catchment area.

It begins as a series of small field ditches but by Plymyard Dale it displays the characteristics of a natural stream for the first time. It flows in a series of small incised meanders, fringed to either side by waterside vegetation. At this point, too, the Dibbin displays one of the problems that it encounters as it flows north alongside heavily built up residential areas. Its banks are badly eroded by trampling, a victim of its very popularity.

As it continues to meander north, the Dibbin captures a small tributary, known as Hargrave Brook, which flows through its own small wooded valley. Beyond this point, the Dibbin joins its main tributary, the Clatter Brook.

The Clatter Brook has appropriated its own tributaries on the way to the Dibbin. Two of these rise in the north, close to the edge of the catchment area near Storeton. Together, they flow south through a predominantly agricultural landscape to be met by a further tributary, Brimstage Brook, which rises at the Heswall hills. The Clatter Brook then moves through the grounds of Clatterbridge Hospital before its confluence with Thornton Brook and Raby Brook at Raby Mere.

The Dibbin enters Dibbinsdale LNR at Poulton Bridge on the Dibbinsdale road. Because of the deepness of the valley at this point, the road descends quite steeply before climbing up towards Poulton. Walking along the route of the Dibbin as it meanders north within the LNR is straightforward, since access paths run alongside it and through Brotherton Park as far as Spital Dam. However, the most dramatic approach to Dibbinsdale is not from the Poulton end or Spital Dam but rather from the entrance to Brotherton Park. Following the trail map, the visitor is suddenly made aware of being on the high ridge of a steep sided and wooded valley. The Dibbin's floodplain appears below but has been made easily accessible on foot. The only element that mars this view are the houses that sit on the ridge of the opposite valley side.

Dibbinsdale contains a variety of landscapes, as well as areas of conservation value. The valley sides are well-wooded with a mixture of waterside and woodland species. The valley floor contains reedbeds and semi-improved grassland as well as the meandering river. It contains parkland where ornamental rhododendrons have begun to take a hold and also sandstone outcrops eroded by the ancient river.

On the final leg of its journey to the Mersey, from Spital Dam to Bromborough Pool, the Dibbin loses its semi-rural nature and adopts the man-made character of the industrial waterfront through which it passes. At Spital Dam, a weir was built to manage the water flow for the now demolished Bromborough water mill. The weir remains but the site of the old mill is now occupied by a sewer pumping station. Throughout this section, the Dibbin has been canalised and reprofiled with flood control, rather than aesthetic, objectives in mind. It passes under the busy A41 Chester Road at the 'white bridge' and between a golf range to one side and the site of the seventeenth century Bromborough Court House on the other. From there, the Dibbin skirts around the Unichema complex and, finally, across the recently filled Bromborough Dock, entering the Mersey over a spillway constructed at the mouth of the former dockgates.

Pond by the Wirral Way,
Thurstaston

Conclusion

The Birket at Bidston

This descriptive account aims no higher than giving a snapshot view of Wirral's rivers and streams. Some of the observations are based purely on personal experience; by following on the ground the detail shown on an Ordnance Survey map and looking, sometimes for the first time, at a section of a particular watercourse. It has been a fascinating process since, by so doing, it has confirmed what seems obvious – that rivers, streams, brooks are all part of a natural, linear system which, if one part is affected, the whole can be affected. This is particularly true when thinking about water quality, but it applies also to flood control and to the richness or otherwise of vegetation and wildlife (such as garden birds) that also move along these water corridors.

Wirral's watercourses do have problems, that is certainly true. They have been culverted, restrained, dumped on, neglected and generally misused. But then, these negative things are not unique to the Wirral. Over recent years, we have become much more aware of the environment and of the need to take care of it if we can. Let us start with Wirral's rivers and streams.

Penny Beckett

The maps

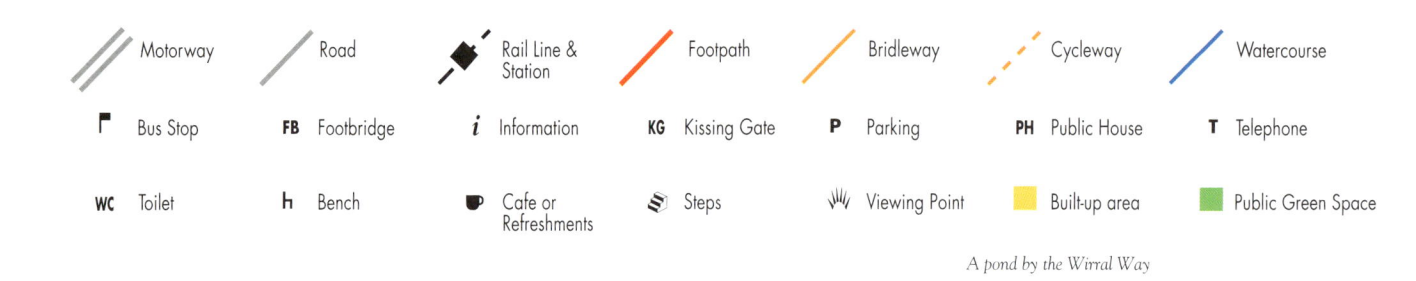

Motorway	Road	Rail Line & Station	Footpath	Bridleway	Cycleway	Watercourse
Bus Stop	FB Footbridge	*i* Information	KG Kissing Gate	P Parking	PH Public House	T Telephone
WC Toilet	h Bench	Cafe or Refreshments	Steps	Viewing Point	Built-up area	Public Green Space

A pond by the Wirral Way

Map locations

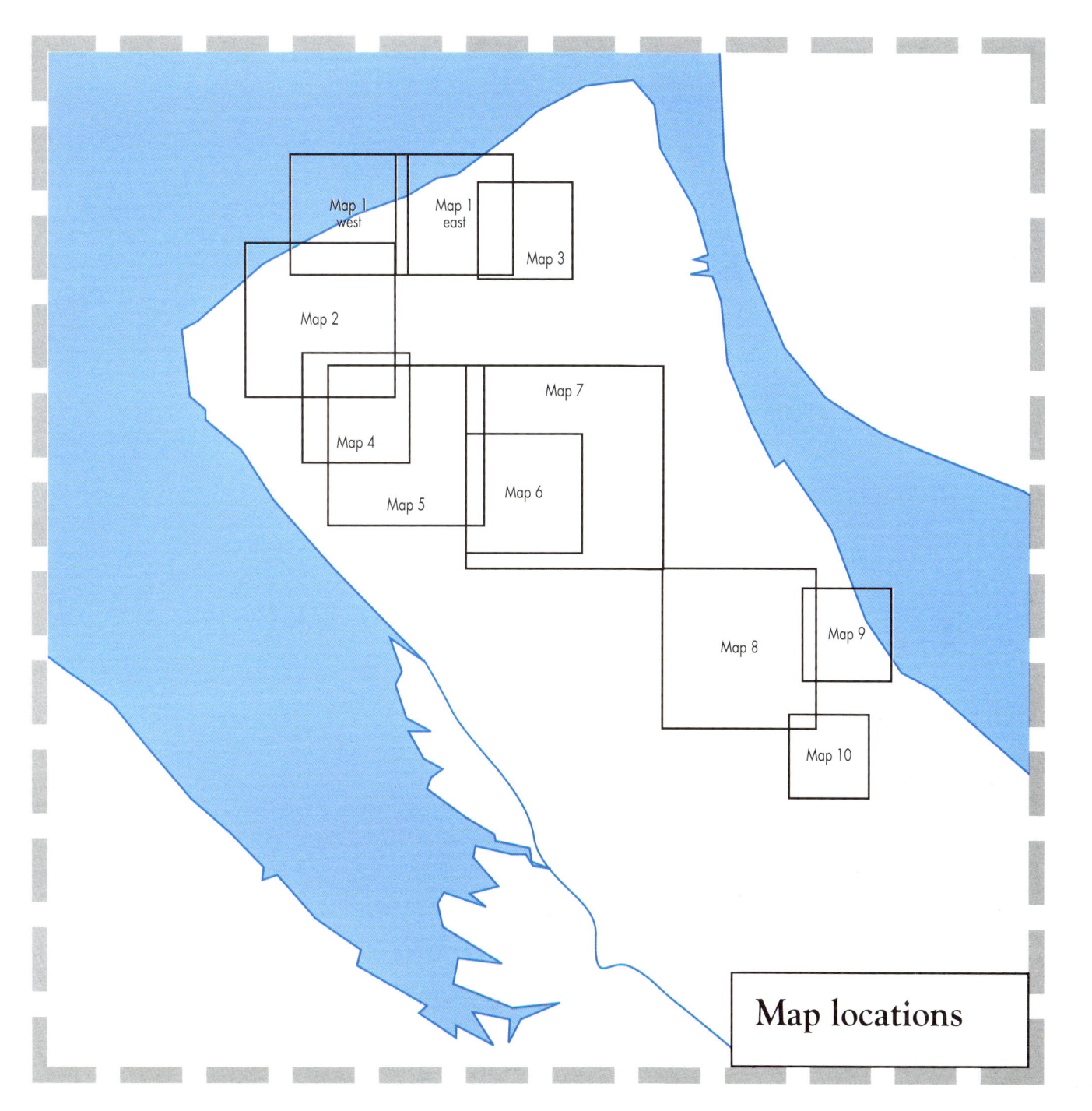

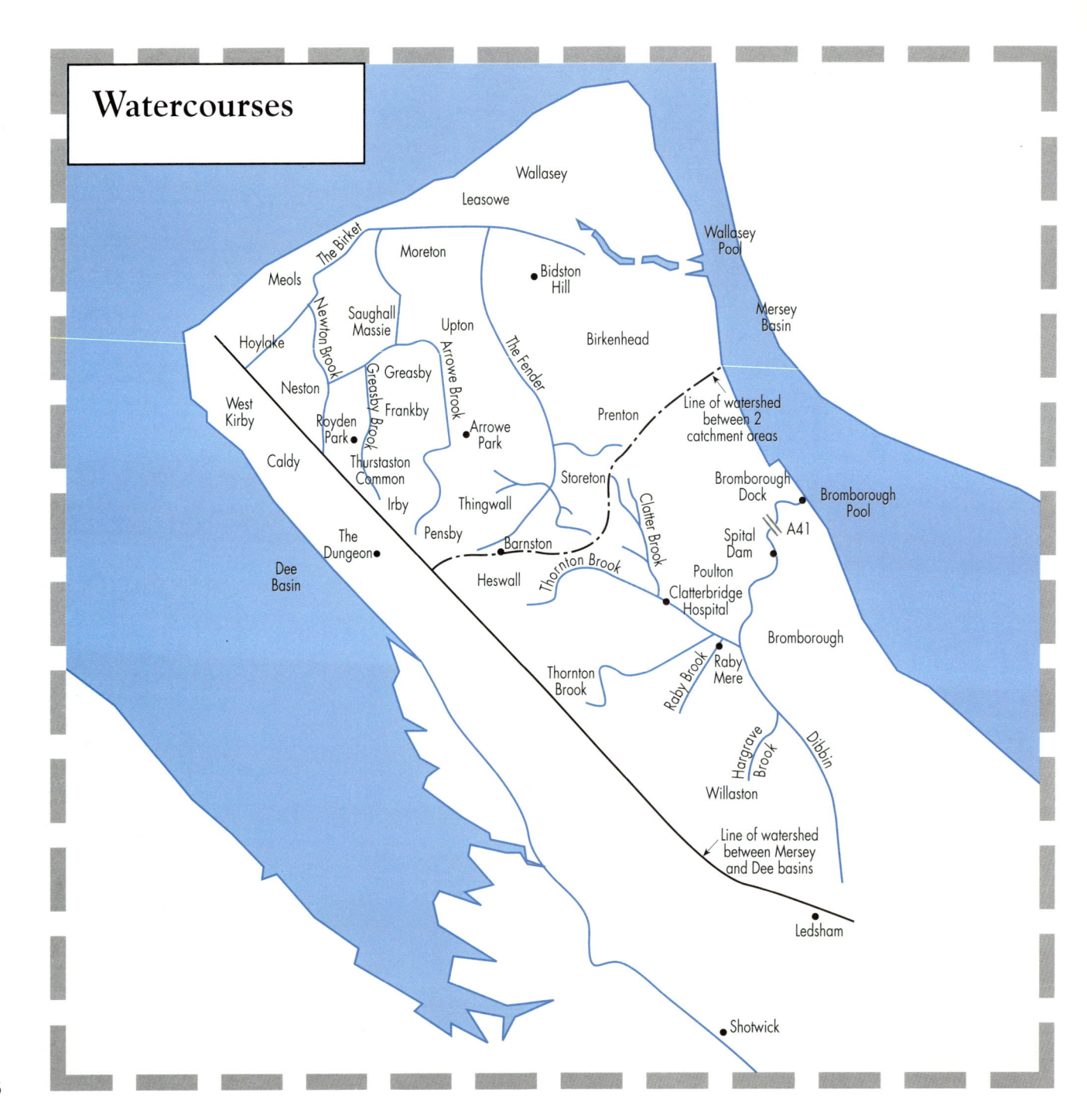

Watercourses

Wildlife locations

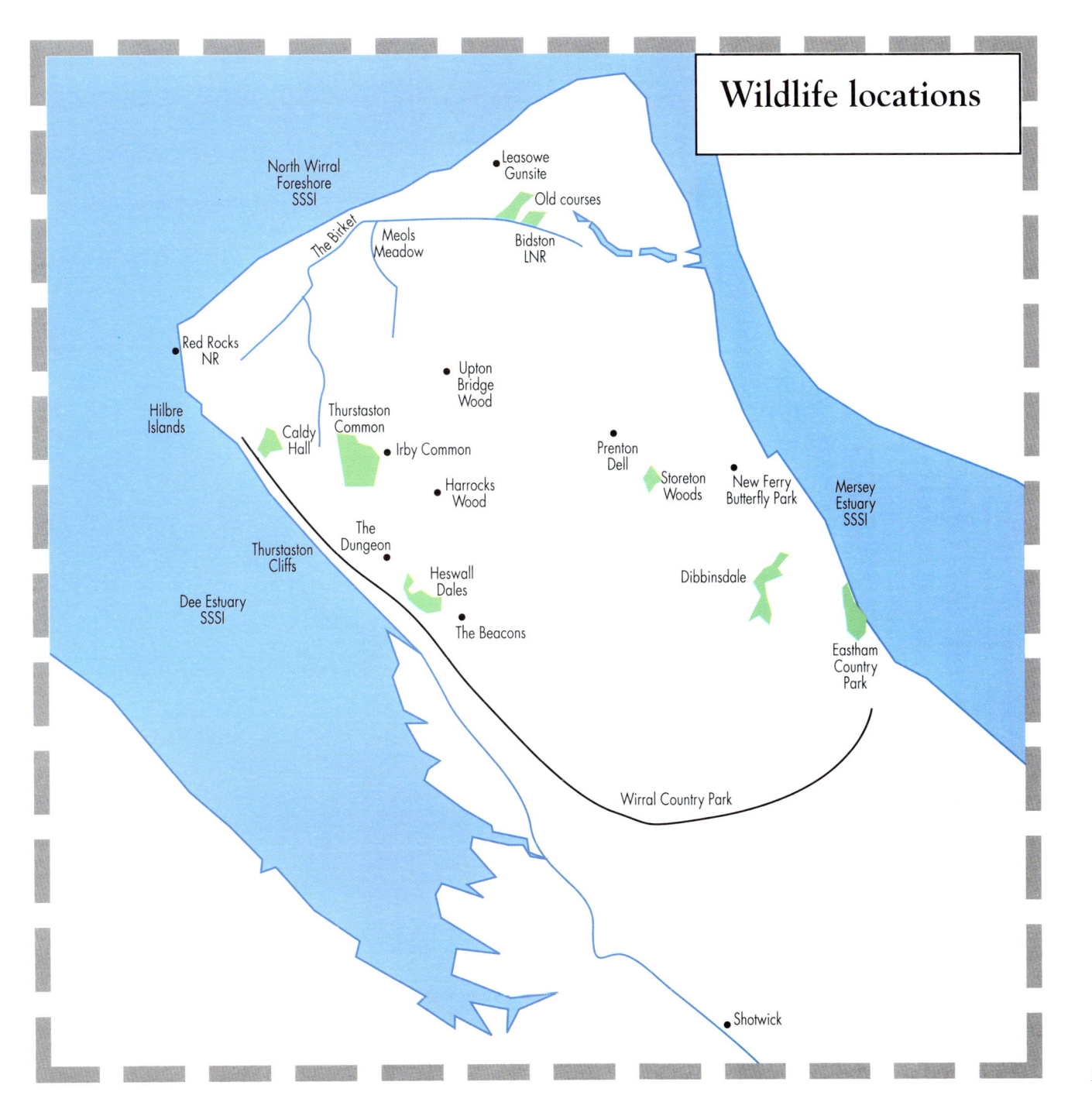

- North Wirral Foreshore SSSI
- Leasowe Gunsite
- Old courses
- The Birket
- Meols Meadow
- Bidston LNR
- Red Rocks NR
- Upton Bridge Wood
- Hilbre Islands
- Caldy Hall
- Thurstaston Common
- Irby Common
- Prenton Dell
- Storeton Woods
- New Ferry Butterfly Park
- Mersey Estuary SSSI
- Harrocks Wood
- The Dungeon
- Thurstaston Cliffs
- Heswall Dales
- Dibbinsdale
- Dee Estuary SSSI
- The Beacons
- Eastham Country Park
- Wirral Country Park
- Shotwick

Map one West

Map one East

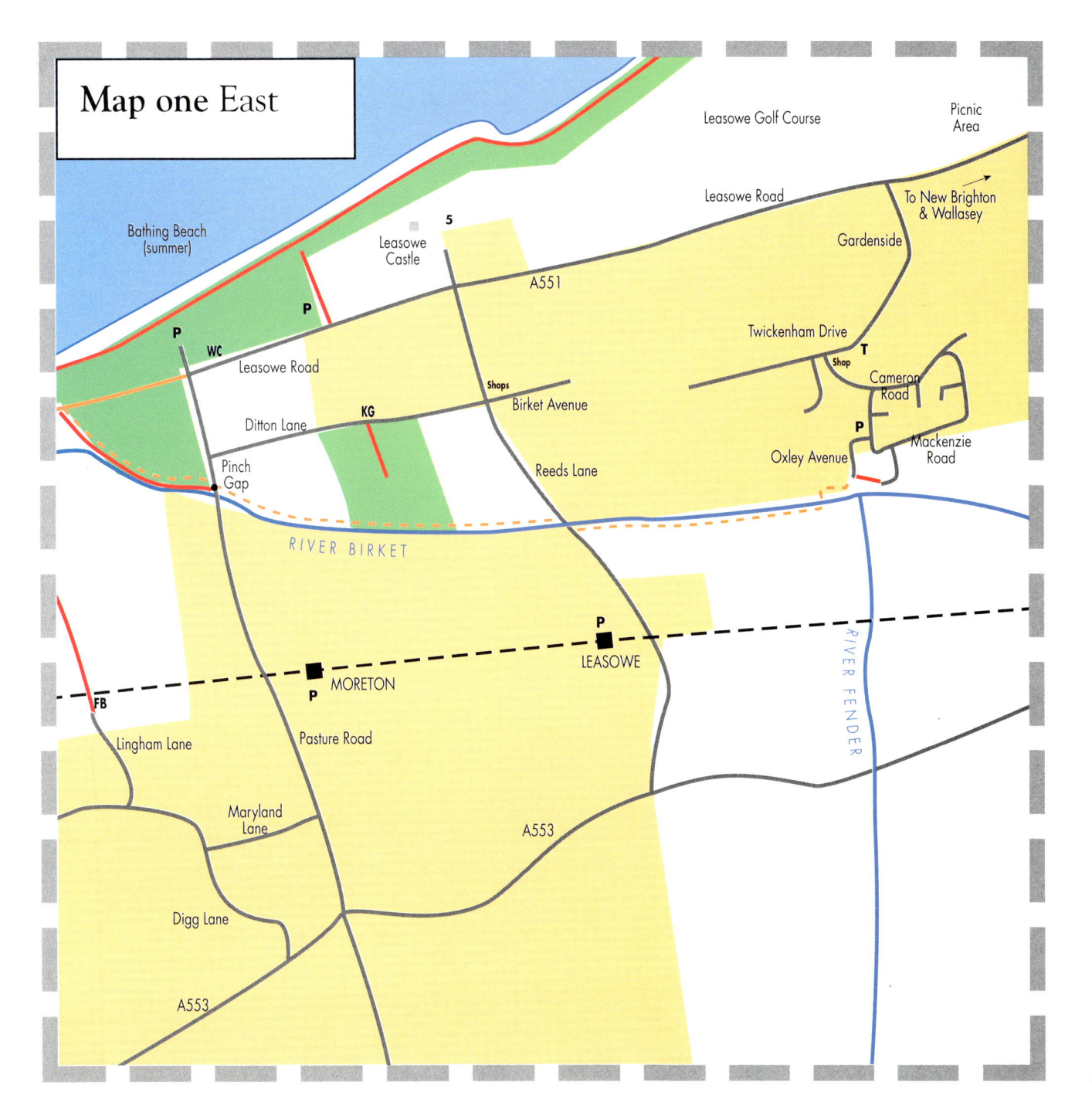

Map one – The Birket is a relatively large river and is maintained for flood control purposes. Without such flood prevention measures, which have included the construction of a sea wall along the North Wirral coast, pumping stations and raised earthbeds, most of the low-lying land of the North Wirral plain would be under water during tidal surges.

Since the need for such flood control is paramount, the Birket is heavily engineered and visually dull as it cuts through an often bleak, windswept landscape. Little vegetation is permitted to grow on its banks and its channel has been deepened and straightened to increase its water-holding capacity. Yet, the open land through which it passes yields up some occasional surprises. One such example of this is the area known as Meols Meadow (1). With its reed beds and ponds fringed with trees and shrubs it sustains lapwings, skylarks and rare flowers.

The North Wirral Coastal Park (2) is over five miles in length and covers some 800 acres of land and foreshore. The actual coastline area is one of Britain's top sites for birdwatching, especially wading birds such as oystercatcher, turnstone and curlew. In recognition of this, the area is a designated site of special scientific interest (SSSI), which legally protects it from industrial development. The coastal path is suitable for wheelchair users and pushchairs

The park's history can be traced back at least 5,000 years, when the area was forested, including parts of what is now the foreshore. The remains of trees, known as the submerged forest, can occasionally be seen at Dove Point (3) between the slipway and the groyne. Evidence of the area being inhabited by people during the stone age has, over the years, been found on the beach in the form of the remains of their houses. (For more information about the park telephone 0151 678 5488)

Close to the park is Leasowe Lighthouse (4) which was built in 1763 by the Liverpool Corporation Docks Committee. The last light was turned off in 1908. After a short period as a tea room the building remained derelict until 1989, when the ground floor of the lighthouse was opened as a visitor centre.

Over the years a group of local people, 'The Friends of Leasowe Lighthouse', have worked towards restoring the building. For example, they removed the remaining dangerous steps from the spiral staircase and replaced them with new cast iron steps, copied from the original pattern. The top floor of the lighthouse was eventually opened to the public in August 1996.

Another landmark in the area is Leasowe Castle (5), built in 1593 by Ferdinando, the 5th Earl of Derby. The original octagonal tower was, it is believed, built as a viewing platform for the famous Wallasey horse race, the forerunner of the Derby race.

To the east, the confluence of the Birket and Arrowe Brook (6) has been canalised and so is very straight with steep grassy banks. Hedges cut off any view of the river until you reach the bridge. Unfortunately, the river on the east of the bridge is very ugly, having upright sheets of iron for banks which lean into the river and have thick concrete 'timbers' horizontally thrust between the banks, spanning the river.

A new cyclepath (7) runs along the river, although the view of the river is obscured by a brick wall where the path first joins the road. The wall is necessary as it prevents cyclists falling in! The remainder of the cycle path along the Birket is planned and will afford a good view of the river and the surrounding attractive land. It is hoped that the path will eventually extend all the way to Bidston Moss.

North Wirral coast looking towards Leasowe Lighthouse

Map two

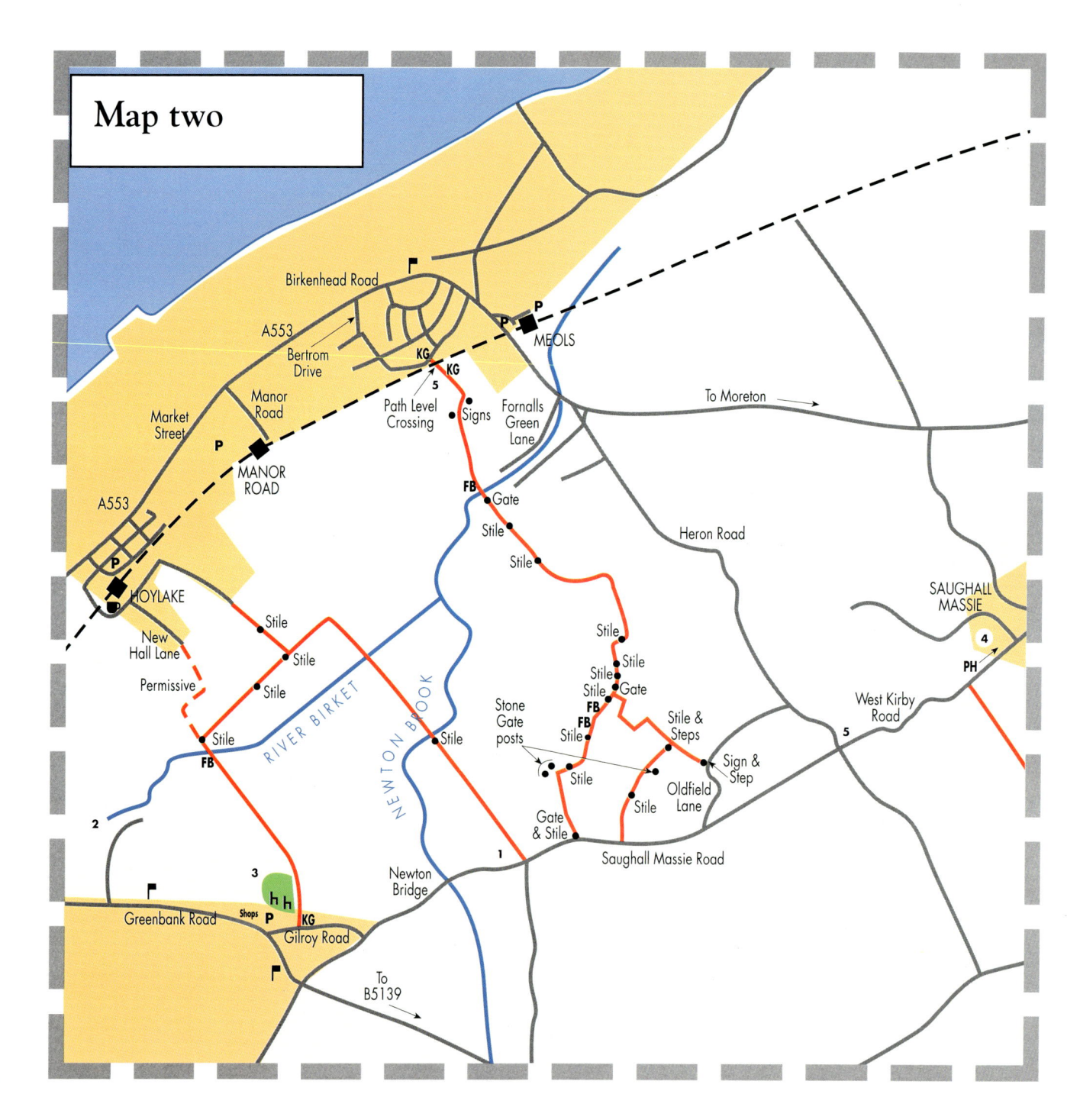

Map two – The two sections of watercourses featured on this map are Newton Brook and River Birket. Although there are plenty of footpaths in the area, wheelchair and pushchair access is limited.

Newton Brook can be observed by wheelchair users at Newton Bridge on Saughall Massie Road and also by following the path which leaves the road a little further along (1).

The source of the Birket is just off Greenbank Road (2) where a stream emerges from under the playing fields. However, it is hard to see the stream because it is surrounded by a pumping station and a high fence. The river can be seen at several other points in this area and can get quite high in winter. It is normally clean and, therefore, able to sustain aquatic life and attract wildfowl which nest and breed along its banks.

Gilroy Nature Park (3) is certainly worth visiting for two very good reasons. Firstly, because of its importance in preserving and promoting conservation and secondly because it illustrates perfectly what RiVa 2005 stands for, i.e. local people protecting their local watercourse and its surrounding environment.

The ground behind the estate at Gilroy Road and Greenbank Road had been used as a rubbish tip for 30 years. In 1982, it was closed and filled in with rubble from demolished high-rise flats and then covered with clay and seeded. Part of the area was designated for agricultural use and part for recreation. The land had always been wet, so it was drained leaving a pond of 2.5 acres with an island in the middle. During a dustman-strike in 1984 the area became very untidy. Local boy Carl Lanceley, who was interested in birdwatching, wanted to improve the area. He persuaded his parents and teachers to become involved and eventually, with the help of a Countryside Ranger, the Gilroy Nature Conservation Society was established.

The Nature Park is managed by the Society, who carry out the necessary conservation tasks and also hold birdwatching meetings and walks. The society have been very successful in attracting many species of birds to breed within the park, for example, Canada goose, dunnock, coot, moorhen, reed bunting and wren. (Gilroy Nature Conservation Society can be contacted on 0151 625 9009)

Also worth a visit is the carefully preserved 18th century hamlet of Saughall Massie(4). 'Saughall' means a hall or slope of willows, 'Massie' is the name of a powerful Wirral family from the Middle Ages. A lot of its buildings date back to the 17th century and are characteristically squat and constructed out of the local red sandstone. These, with the working farms of the village help Saughall Massie maintain its country atmosphere.

At Three Lanes End (5) the lane running towards Meols is thought to be part of a Roman road. Such a road ran from Chester in this direction and traces of the route have been found in other parts of Wirral.

All these paths cross rolling grassy fields and small watercourses. Wherever you are there's a feel of 'being in the country', making any walk a nice day out that could be rounded off with a pub lunch at Meols, Saughall Massie, Hoylake or West Kirby.

Map three

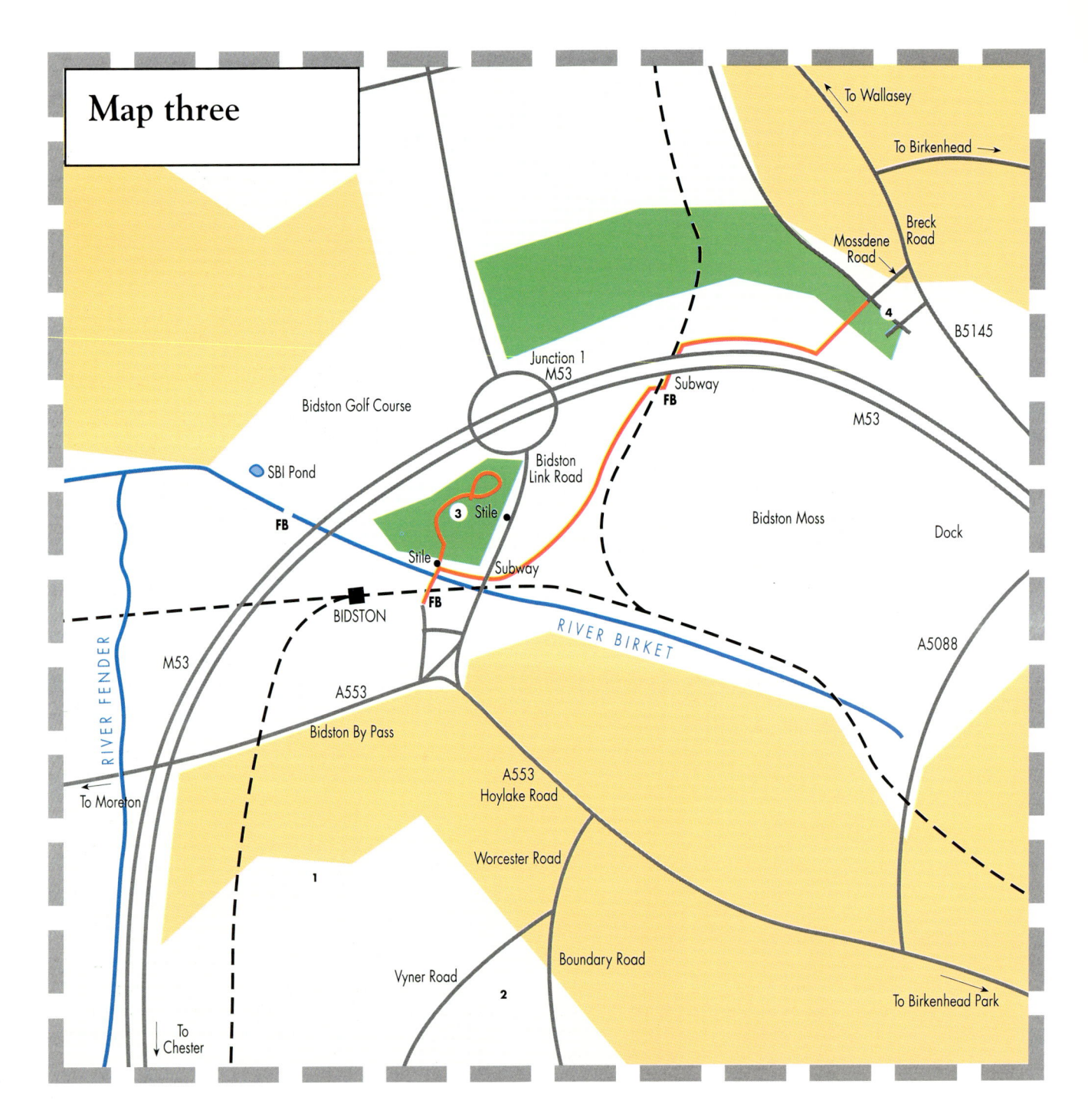

The marshlands and reedbeds provide an excellent habitat for a vast selection of birds including the sedge warbler

Map three – The River Birket on this map is visually very unappealing. It has been heavily engineered, with steep grassy banks and deep channels dug to prevent flooding It also shows signs of pollution from the various urban developments in the area.

It's not all bad news though, there are several places of interest. On Bidston Hill (1) there is an observatory and a lighthouse, both built in the mid 1800s. There is also a well restored windmill which was built in the late 18th century. It is believed that there has, for the most part, been a windmill on this site since 1596. (for more information contact the Tam O'Shanter Farm, telephone 0151 653 9332) From the top of the hill you can get a great view over the Fender Valley.

Built around 300 years ago, Tam O'Shanter Cottage (2) has had a chequered history. It is now an urban farm where people, especially children, can come and get close to the various animals and see the day-to-day workings of a city farm.

In 1837, local stonemason Richard Leary, the tenant at the time, decorated the exterior of the cottage with scenes from Burns' poem 'Tam O'Shanter'. The poem tells of how Tam, pursued by witches, crossed the bridge, knowing that they would not cross running water. He escaped, but his mare Maggie lost her tail.

The farm was almost completely destroyed by fire in 1954, but it was saved by public protest only to be the victim of another fire sixteen years later in 1970. Following this, it was decided that the cottage should be demolished but the Birkenhead History Society won permission to fully restore it in order to open it to the public. It has been open to schools and other youth organisations since 1977.

Bidston Moss Local Nature Reserve (3) has been designated as such since 1994. The right of way from Mosslands Drive towards Bidston was once the only safe route across the marshy land of Bidston Moss. Land drainage and the canalisation of the River Birket has since allowed buildings to be erected.

Ponds, paths and boardwalks have been constructed in the reserve over the last thirteen years. Access is limited to pedestrians only, due to a stile access close to Bidston Railway. But this only applies to the nature reserve west of A554. There are no stiles on the right of way and by mid 1998 this footpath will be a cycle way

The reserve is home to rich and varied wildlife and as such it has been a Site of Biological Interest since 1980. In particular, the marshland and reedbeds provide an excellent habitat for a vast selection of birds. For example warblers, little grebe and various birds of prey. Heron are also regularly seen in and around the ponds. Although most of the path is unattractive, these surrounding features make a visit worthwhile.

The paths shown on this map pass mostly through agricultural land, providing pleasant strolls. It is the variety of birds and habitats which make a visit to the Hill and Woods a pleasure.

Map four

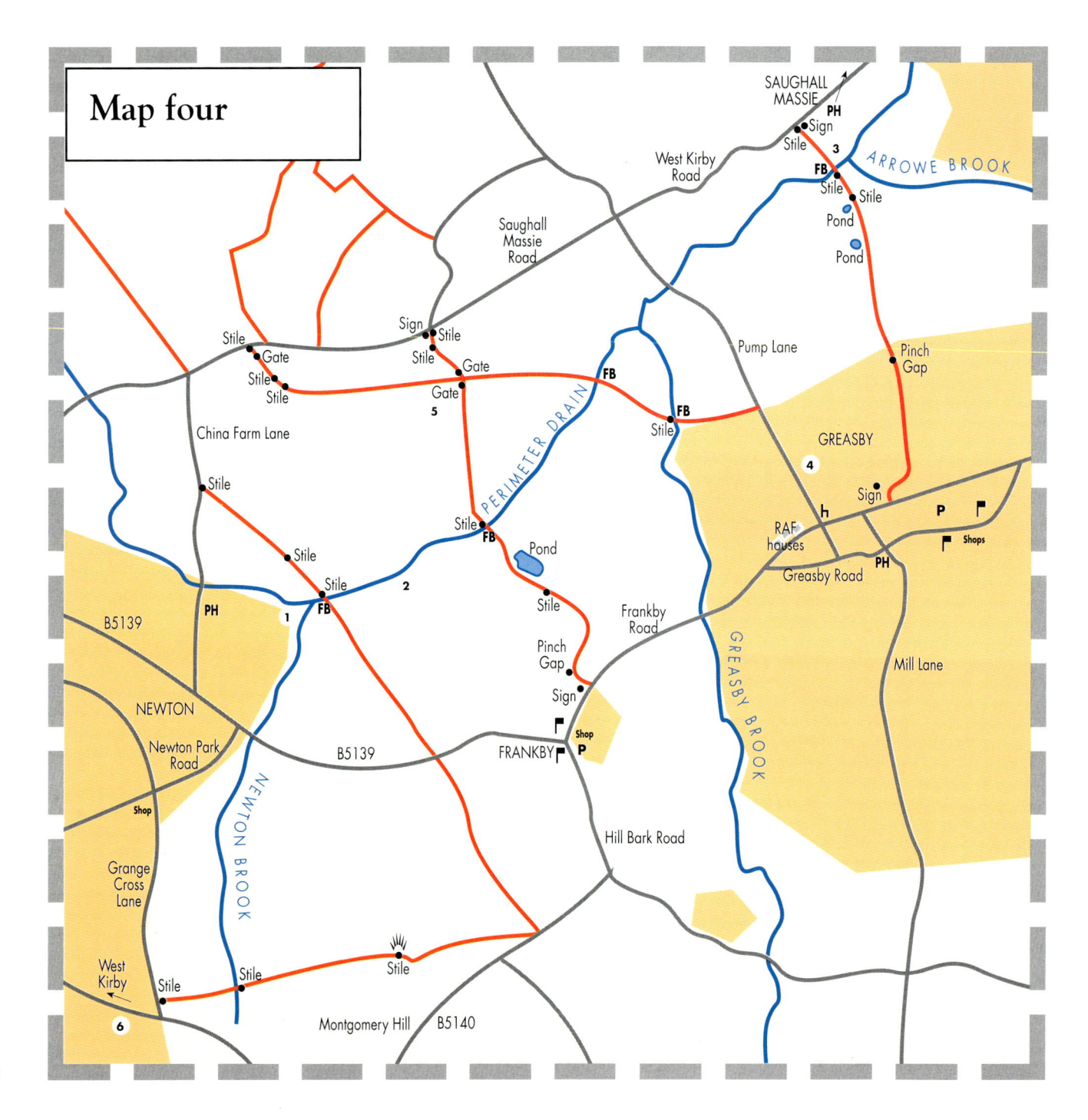

Map four — There are several interesting features on the watercourses in this area. At the confluence of the Perimeter Drain and Newton Brook (1) there is a large willow tree which fell down just a couple of years ago causing the brook to turn sharply in the nook of its roots. This picturesque point on the brook is accessible by wheelchair users, via the path from Montgomery Hill, up to the footbridge at the confluence.

To the east of the confluence (2) there is a point at which the Perimeter Drain flows in opposite directions! This is due to the land in the area being virtually flat and therefore the small amount of water in the drain runs from the land very slowly. Having said this, it should be noted that the Perimeter Drain normally runs completely dry during the summer.

Much of the land around the footpath, which heads north from Frankby Road to West Kirby Road, is used informally, for dog-walking etc. Because of these extra tracks, it is easy to stray from the designated footpath. As a way of getting back on the correct path, if you are heading towards West Kirby Road and you reach a watercourse (3) but there is no footbridge, look at the direction the water is flowing. If it is from right to left, you're at Arrowe Brook and you need to turn left. If it's flowing from left to right, you're at Greasby Brook and you need to turn right.

The nearest amenities to those paths are at Saughall Massie and Greasby, the name of which is thought to be Anglo-Saxon. At the time of the Domesday Survey, the village was known as Gravesberie. In the 1800s, when infectious diseases were rampant, Greasby Library was used as an isolation hospital during an outbreak of smallpox. At Pump Lane there is the old pump and pond (4) which originally supplied the village with its water.

A footpath from Saughall Massie Road takes you into an area which used to be an RAF training base (5). It didn't train pilots, so there weren't any planes! However, the footpaths are now open to the public; follow the lines of the roads which were the arteries of the base.

At the bottom left of this map (6), you will find Caldy Hill and Stapledon Wood. Caldy Hill is an area of lowland heath and mixed deciduous woodland, located on a sandstone outcrop with fine views across the Dee Estuary and towards the Isle of Man in clear weather.

A major landmark at the hill is the Mariners Beacon which stands on the site of an old windmill, which was a very useful aid to maritime navigation. When it was destroyed by a gale in 1839, it was greatly missed and consequently the trustees of the Liverpool Docks erected the Beacon in 1841.

The heathland is of regional significance with varieties of heather including cross leafed and bell heather. The gorse and bracken with birch and oak scrub provide good cover for various birds, small animals and foxes.

Stapledon Wood is a mixed plantation of oak, sweet chestnut, beech, ash, elm and sycamore. During the spring, the wood contains masses of bluebells and daffodils, making it very beautiful. Through the summer, the trees support a variety of woodland birds such as woodpecker, nuthatch and treecreeper. Summer migrants include spotted flycatcher and warblers. Pied flycatchers and wood warblers have started arriving in recent summers.

Map five

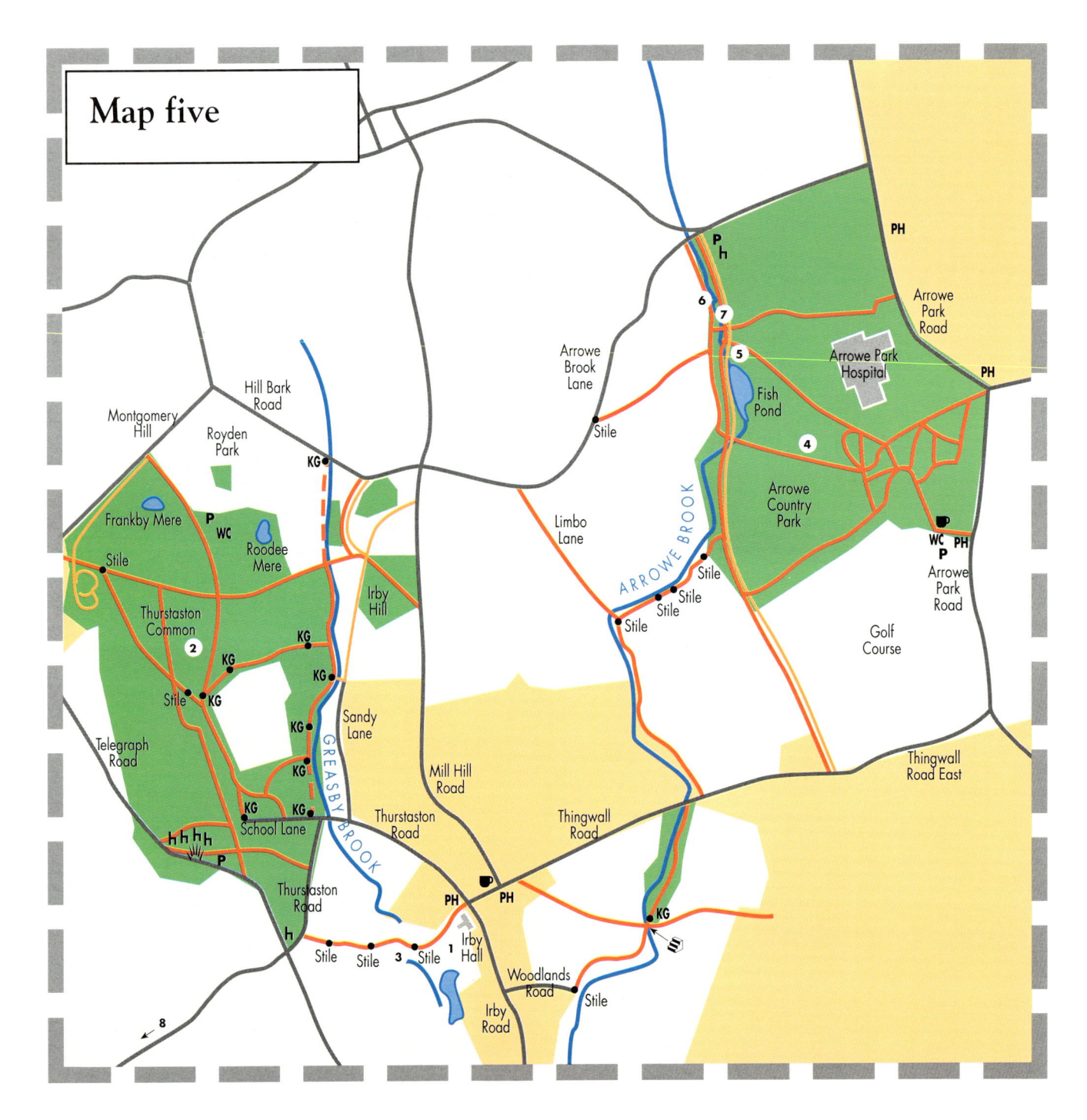

Herons are a common sight around water areas

Map 5 – The two brooks focused on in this section, Greasby Brook and Arrowe Brook, arise only a field away from each other at Irby.

The Greasby Brook's source is near to a large pond at the rear of Irby Hall (1), from there it flows northwards along the edge of Thurstaston Common (2) to Frankby and then off this map towards Greasby. The stream is clean, but often runs dry during the summer months.

An ancient well site known as Londymere and a mediaeval boundary stone allude to the importance of the brook in the 'bounds' of Irby and Thurstaston during an early boundary dispute between Lord Thurstaston and the Abbott of Saint Wherburgh. Although the stone remains in the area (3), don't be disappointed if you can't locate it, as it is camouflaged by the roots of an old birch tree.

There are plenty of paths in the vicinity and although unsurfaced they offer fairly easy walking. However, the access is often through kissing gates and stiles and so unsuitable for wheelchair users and pushchairs. The good news is that there are plans to improve the route between Sandy Lane, Irby and Royden Park.

Until the mid-nineteenth century, the site of Royden Park was still largely farmland. However, by 1844, there were in existence, areas of tree plantation which were to form the basis of a park landscape which still exist today. The present house of Hillbark was erected in 1931 by Sir Ernest B. Royden, after whom the park is named. The mock-Tudor building, originally known as Bidston Court, was built near Bidston Hill for the soap manufacturer R.W. Hudson and then moved, brick by brick, about four miles to its present location.

The parkland around the house offers a range of wildlife habitats with its deciduous and coniferous woodland, grass meadow and fresh water. The two rhododendron-lined meres offer nesting sites for moorhen, mallard and Canada geese.

The Arrowe Brook is also relatively clean and therefore home to a variety of wildlife; invertebrate life is rich in its upper sections.

It is accessible at several points; the footpath from Irby, via Harrock Wood is accessible by stiles, although there are steep steps on one of the stream crossings. From Thingwall Road you can follow the brook upstream through Harrock Wood, or downstream into Arrowe Country Park (4).

For easier access to the park, start from Thingwall Road East or Arrowe Brook Road car park. Apart from one short stretch, which can become muddy in the rain, the paths are hard surfaced and therefore generally suitable for all users.

About half of the park's 400 acres is open parkland, the remainder being used for an 18 hole municipal golf course. The brook and the numerous ponds, together with the grass and woodland accommodate all sorts of wildlife, from butterflies and dragonflies, to kingfishers and newts.

The park was purchased by John Shaw, a ship owner who made much of his money from the slave trade. His great-nephew John (Nicholson) Shaw inherited the estate and was responsible for most of the landscaping in the park, including the diversion of the brook to provide a source of water for the lake (5).

There is also an oxbow lake on the brook (6), although this is a recent feature. One of the meanders was badly undercutting a large beech tree and, in an attempt to save it, the meander was cut off, so creating the oxbow lake.

Another recent feature is the drain from Arrowe Park Hospital into the Arrowe Brook (7). This originates in the laundry at the hospital and is carefully monitored. Despite the image it conjures up, it is an interesting point at which to observe the brook, upstream the brook babbles and twists over exposed sandstone

The Brook continues out of the park and after a short stretch of copse, enters Upton Meadow. This site has recently been leased to the Woodland Trust, after years of campaigning by local residents to stop it being developed as an industrial estate. The bridleway, which can be used by horse riders, follows the brook but there are many tracks all through the site. These can be used to visit the hay meadow, which has an abundance of flowers and is sometimes home to skylarks – a rare treat this far into Wirral. Also in the site are woods and ponds, and there are plans to put in benches, information boards, hedges and more woods.

Although not actually on this map, Wirral Country Park and The Dungeon (8) are well worth visiting. Head for the 60ft high boulder clay cliffs in the country park and look out over the Dee Estuary and you'll be able to feel the sea-breeze, taste the salt and get a wonderful sense of space. Visit on a clear day and you can see the familiar outline of Moel Famau in the Clwydian Hills.

The Dungeon is best reached from Wirral Country Park at Thurstaston. From here a 3/4 mile walk along the Wirral Way will bring you to the steep sided wooded valley, located on a small stream which flows westerly into the Dee. The area has been designated an SSSI since 1987. This is due to its interesting and important geological exposures; that is, the Triassic system of rocks which was laid down across Wirral 230 million years ago.

As you enter the valley there is a fault in the rock just as the steep part of the valley sides become narrow. The best way to see it is to walk upstream for ten to fifteen feet, however, the rocks along the bank can be slippery, so great care should be taken.

Reedmace at Frankby Mere, Royden Park

Map six

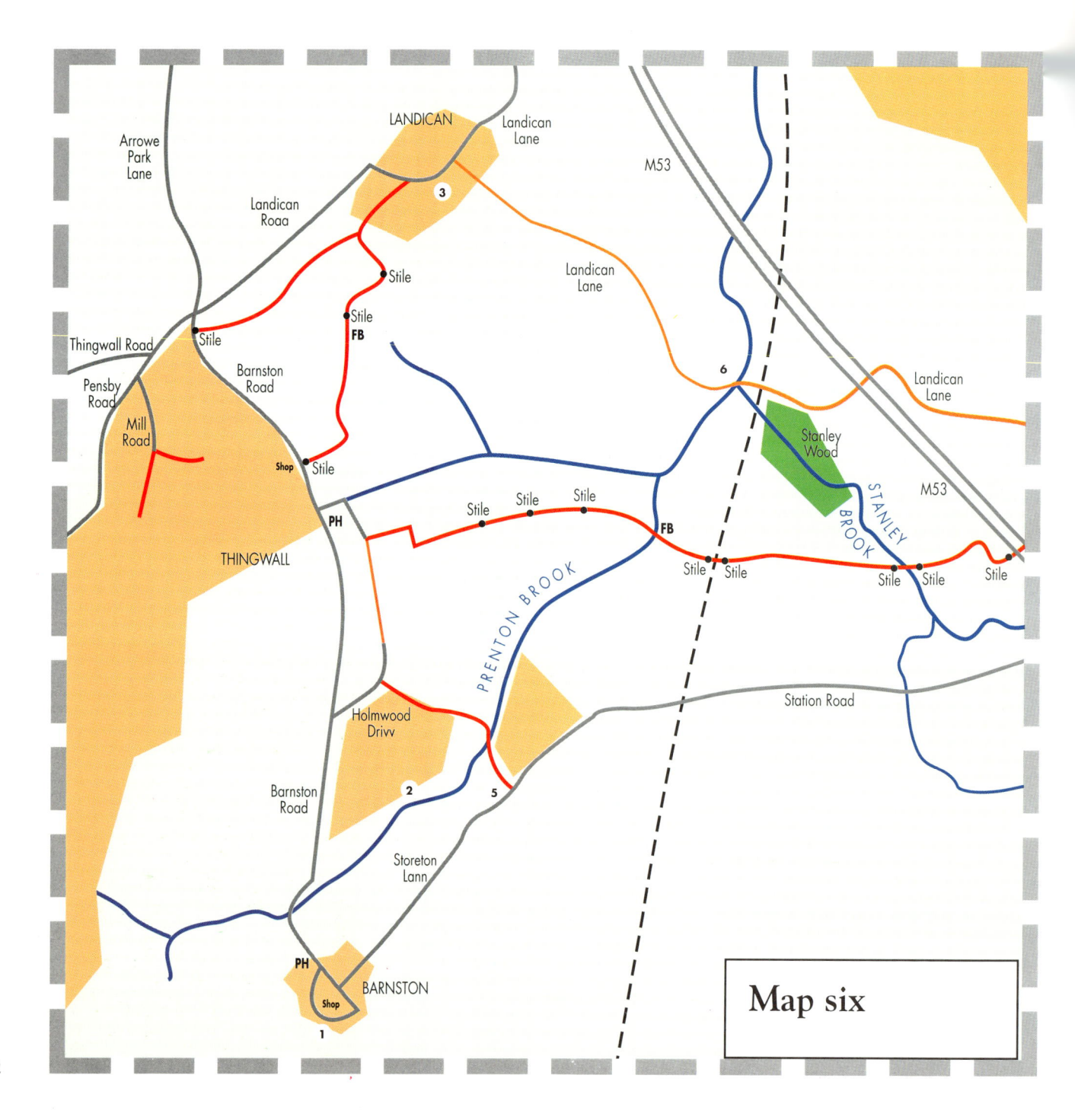

The bee orchid is only found in one or two meadows in the Wirral

Map six – In this section, the River Fender, Prenton Brook and Stanley Brook can be enjoyed. There are also two attractive villages in the area, Barnston and Landican.

Barnston (1) is a rural village; the name derivation varies considerably, but is most probably Anglo-Saxon or Norse. Probably its most picturesque area is Barnston Dale (2), a Site of Biological Interest (SBI), with Prenton Brook trickling through it. It is clean and runs for most of the year, except when there is a drought. With its overhanging banks, steep rocky sides and dense vegetation, the brook provides an excellent habitat for small mammals, including water vole. The dale is particularly pretty in spring when bluebells carpet the deep wooded valley.

Further upstream where the footbridge crosses the brook, there are some examples of very old oak trees. Sadly they are in extremely poor condition. The good news is that, at least, young beech and elder have begun to grow there.

Stanley Brook is also clean, but the section you can see from the footbridge is sometimes dry in summer. A reasonable variety of wildlife can be seen in this area. Signs of rabbit can be frequently found, squirrels may also be seen, as they nest in the hollow trunks of the oaks.

Landican (3) is an incredibly small village with no shops, pubs or even a church. Strange then that the name 'Landican' derives from the Gaelic language, meaning 'church of the oak'. There has never been a church in the area, but, at the time of the Domesday Survey, a priest lived there!

Back to the 20th century, a bridleway (called Landican Lane) runs from Landican across Prenton Brook. At present, the amount of stiles in the area make some of the paths inaccessible to wheelchair users and pushchairs. Prenton Brook can be seen by all visitors from a path which runs from Storeton Lane up to Holmwood Drive (5). Landican Lane bridleway is accessible from Storeton Village up to the brook, making it another point at which all visitors may enjoy the natural meandering stream and is part of the Millennium Cycle Route which runs from Landican to the village of Storeton. This path is planned to be surfaced and will therefore be suitable for wheelchairs.

Map seven

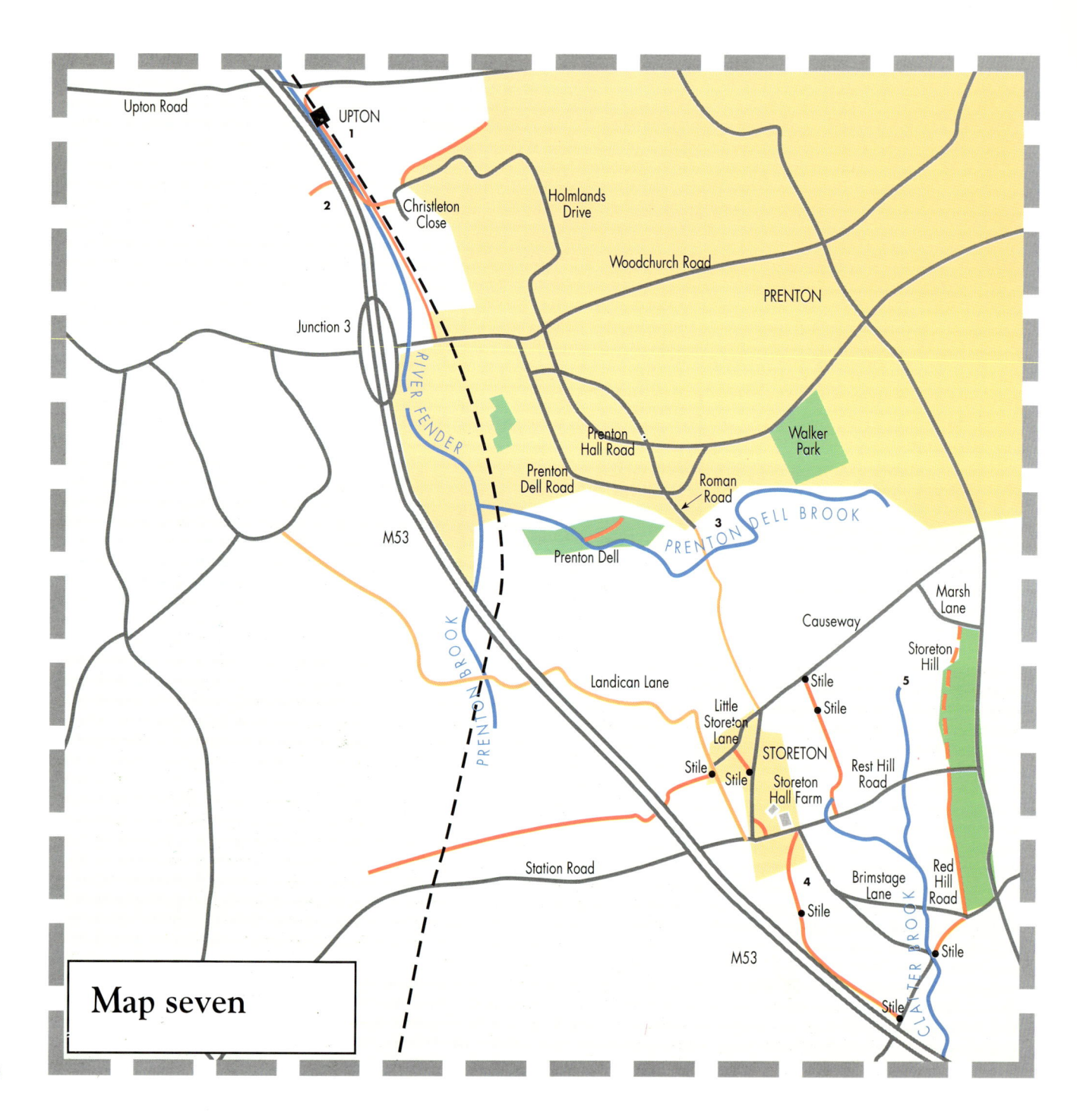

Map seven — There are three watercourses in this area, the Fender, Prenton Dell Brook and the upper part of the Clatter Brook. The section of Fender on this map is typical, in that it runs parallel to the M53, taking second place to the railway line and industrial sites.

South of Upton Station (1), the river is culverted and therefore quite ugly. This can be observed from the footpath which runs alongside it. The entrance to the footpath has recently been upgraded, the dumped rubbish has been removed and a low maintenance wildflower meadow has been established. Further improvements have and indeed continue to be made to this section of the Fender. One such initiative is large scale tree planting (2). To date, 27,000 trees have been planted by local people from Beechwood and Woodchurch. A small amount of wildlife can be seen in this area, such as magpies, kestrels and certain varieties of butterflies.

Also proposed, but not yet finally agreed, is the Millennium Cycle Route. It will follow the line of the M53 from Bidston through Beechwood and across Upton Bypass (not on this map). It then follows onto this map through Woodchurch, crossing to reach Landican Lane and down to Storeton (for more information contact Groundwork Wirral, telephone 0151 666 2424)

Prenton Dell Brook can be seen at Prenton Dell. The brook can also be seen at the end of Roman Road, where a bridleway begins and runs to Storeton. Just beyond the Dell is Prenton Hall Farm and Lower Farm (3), which include the remains of the old hamlet of Prenton.

The village of Storeton (4), the name of which derives from the Anglo-Saxon era, has quite a number of interesting places, not least the source of the Clatter Brook (5). Parts of the buildings of Storeton Hall Farm date back over 600 years to 1360, when it was Storeton Hall, seat of the Stanley family.

Close to the upper part of the Clatter Brook is Storeton Hill, a public greenspace. On the other side of the hill (just off the map) is a building erected in 1865 by a wealthy ship-owner, Sir Thomas Brocklebank. Originally a school, it now serves as a church. It is interesting to browse around as it has managed to retain many of its original features.

Frogs are commonly found in all types of pond

Map eight

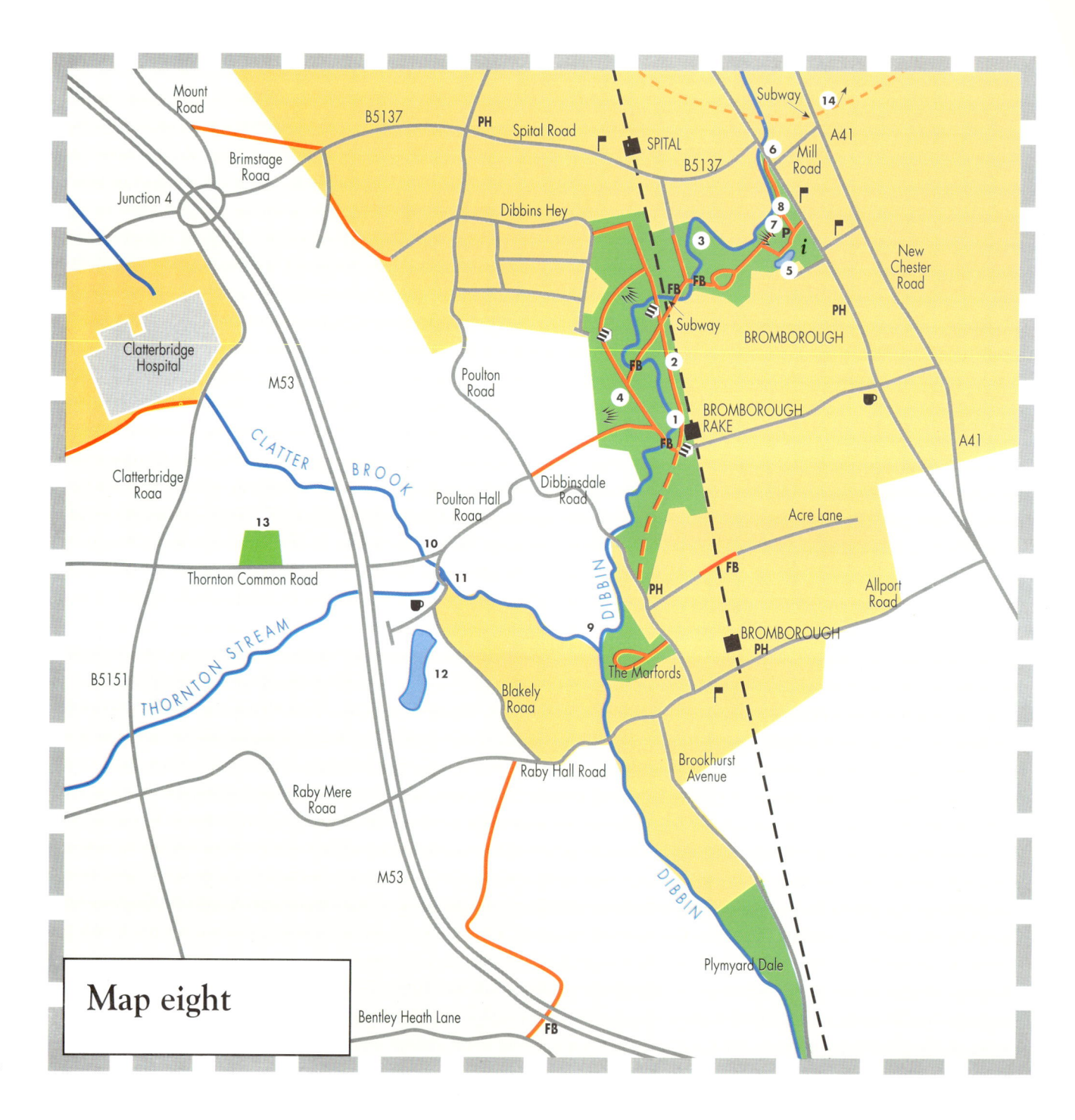

Map eight – The River Dibbin rises on farmland around the village of Ledsham in Cheshire. It flows for about 15 kms, crossing into Merseyside at Eastham. A meandering lowland river, it is allowed to find a natural course, which may change in the valley with time. During flooding, the water levels frequently increase by several metres, immersing some of the surrounding reedbed and grassland.

The Dibbin exhibits many classic landscape features of a mature river valley. While there are no full formations of ox-bow lakes on the Dibbin, some of the smaller meanders are showing signs of ox-bow development. A series of meanders is accessible from the footpath below Bromborough Rake railway station (1). The larger meanders are surrounded by wet or boggy ground and so are inaccessible.

The river is mostly unengineered and vibrant with natural vegetation, which makes it very scenic. At several points along the river it is easy to forget the urban and suburban surroundings, particularly in the valley.

Along its course, the Dibbin is joined by the Clatter Brook and Thornton Stream and flows through, or close to a number of important sites, including the Wirral Way and the Dibbinsdale Local Nature Reserve (LNR). Brotherton Park and Dibbinsdale were designated as an LNR by the Borough Council in 1983. The title holds no legal protection but it demonstrates the strong commitment of the Borough Council to conservation. There is also commitment and respect from the local people, who have managed to reduce damage to the reserve from vandalism and litter.

Dibbinsdale LNR contains the largest block of semi-natural ancient woodland (2) in the region. Together with the reed-beds (3) and meadow grassland (4), this makes it one of Wirral's finest environmental assets. Examples of just some of the wildlife which may be seen in the area are heron, snipe, watervole, teal along with various species of wildflower and butterfly. The ancient woodland is particularly attractive in spring and early summer when bluebells, wood anemone and dogs mercury thrive.

Within the LNR you will find the Ranger's office and the new Brotherton Nature Study Centre (5), which has been built at Woodslee Cottages with financial support from the Brotherton Trust. Until 1993, the buildings and walled garden stood empty and derelict. Lord Brotherton of Wakefield originally purchased the estate in 1919 with the intention of setting up a chemical research laboratory under the name of Port Rainbow. However, due to cheap imports from Germany after World War One, he changed his mind and converted the cottages into servants quarters and stables for Woodslee House.

Most of the footpaths in this area are surfaced but, for all that, the terrain can be steep and, as a general piece of advice, therefore unsuitable for wheelchair users and pushchairs without considerable effort. The best access for wheelchair users is via Woodslee Pond and into the valley, The Ranger Service can help and advise on this.

There is an access point to a footpath off Spital Road which will take you close to the site where, until recently, an ancient watermill stood (6); there was also a windmill nearby at Mill Road.

Downstream, the river has cut through the surface layer of boulder clay, left after the retreat of the last Ice Age and into Triassic bunter sandstone (7). Near-by is Patrick's Well (8), legend has it that it was blessed by Saint Patrick during a visit to the area in 432 AD. It is reputed that the water has healing properties for the eyes, though it is not recommended that you put this to the test!

A footpath off Dibbinsdale Road will take you through the Marfords, where you can observe the point at which the Clatter Brook and River Dibbin Join (9). The Marfords is a small 'enclosed' site alongside the Dibbin with the confluence of the Clatter Brook and the Dibbin at the western end. It is accessible from Dibbinsdale Road, close to the bottom end of Dibbinsdale LNR. Unfortunately this path is unsuitable for wheelchair users due to very steep paths and uneven terrain. (Contact Dibbindale LNR for information, telephone 0151 334 9851)

Moving north-west towards the confluence of Thornton Stream and Clatter Brook (10), there is further ancient woodland (11), unfortunately it is on private land. It is also a Cheshire Wildlife Trust reserve and therefore has no public access to it. Indeed, public access in this area is very limited, including that to Raby Mere (12). Although the mere is a great spot to view ducks, swans and other waterfowl, there is access to the roadside only. However, there is access to Thornton Common (13) from Thornton Common Road where small ponds and the surrounding woodland can be enjoyed.

To the north of the Dibbin, is the world famous Port Sunlight Village (14). In 1887, William Hesketh Lever, a successful soap manufacturer, began looking for a new site for his factory. He needed land on which to build his new works and have space for expansion. The site also needed to be near a river for importing raw materials and a railway line for transporting the finished products. The marshy, uninspiring ground that he discovered was eventually to be transformed into the village, which was named after his famous Sunlight Soap.

Production began at Port Sunlight in 1889 and has continued virtually without interruption ever since. The plant now consists of four self-contained factories, two for liquids, one for soaps and one a sulphonation plant.

Port Sunlight is now a conservation area, still within its original boundaries, although now it is not necessary to be an employee or pensioner of a Unilever company to qualify for residence in the village. (Port Sunlight Heritage Centre can be contacted on 0151 64 6466)

Foxes can be seen in many areas around the Wirral

Map nine

Map nine – In 1086, when the Domesday Survey was collated, Eastham was described as the largest and most valuable place in Wirral. This was most probably due to its excellent geographical position on the River Mersey.

Later, during the Middle Ages, a ferry service began operating across the River Mersey between Eastham and Liverpool, the early ferries being run by monks from the Abbey of Saint Wherburgh in Chester. However, by the 1840s, the demand for it declined as a railway link between Chester and Woodside Perry Terminal, at Birkenhead, became more popular.

In 1846, Eastham Ferry Hotel was built, and, shortly after, the pleasure gardens were added to attract more visitors. A sandstone jetty (1) opposite the hotel is the remains of the ferry landing stage, built in 1878. The small building close to the jetty was once the ticket office where visitors. could book their trip on one of the paddle steamers, either 'Ruby', 'Pearl' or 'Sapphire.'

Further prosperity was brought to the area when the Manchester Ship Canal was opened in 1894 by Queen Victoria.

Eastham soon became know as the 'Richmond of the Mersey.' Unfortunately, its popularity declined during the 1920s until finally the last ferry made its crossing in 1929.

Forty years later, in 1970, the area was designated as Eastham Country Park, and is today, once again, a highly attractive place. Situated adjacent to the Mersey and close to the Manchester Ship Canal entrance, it possesses some splendid examples of natural history including around 100 acres of mature broad leaf woodland and cliffs which provide excellent views over the internationally recognised Mersey Estuary, where flocks of waders and ducks can be seen.

Along with the wildfowl, many other birds are attracted to the park at various times of the year, including nuthatches, tree-creepers, sparrowhawk and all three types of woodpecker. This is due mainly to the abundance of berries, nuts and invertebrates which are available as a source of food.

Several species of bat live at Eastham Country Park, but as they are obviously nocturnal, they are not usually seen. This is the same with most of the mammals in the park, for example foxes, hedgehogs, woodmice and weasels. One mammal which does make its existence known is the grey squirrel; they are now so tame that they will accept any food you may offer.

Access routes in the park are good. Surfaced paths along the river front are prolific and despite there being a few shallow slopes, wheelchair users should be able to manage them.

There are plenty of public amenities in the park, such as a visitors' centre, Rangers' office, toilets and shops (2). There are also two pubs which are situated on the river front.

Public access is constantly being upgraded and improved in this area just as it is all over Wirral. This map shows the route of a planned cycleway (3) which will link the park to Spital Road (map 8). It is due to be open to the public in 1998.

(For more information, contact Eastham Country Park Rangers, telephone 0151 327 1007)

Map ten

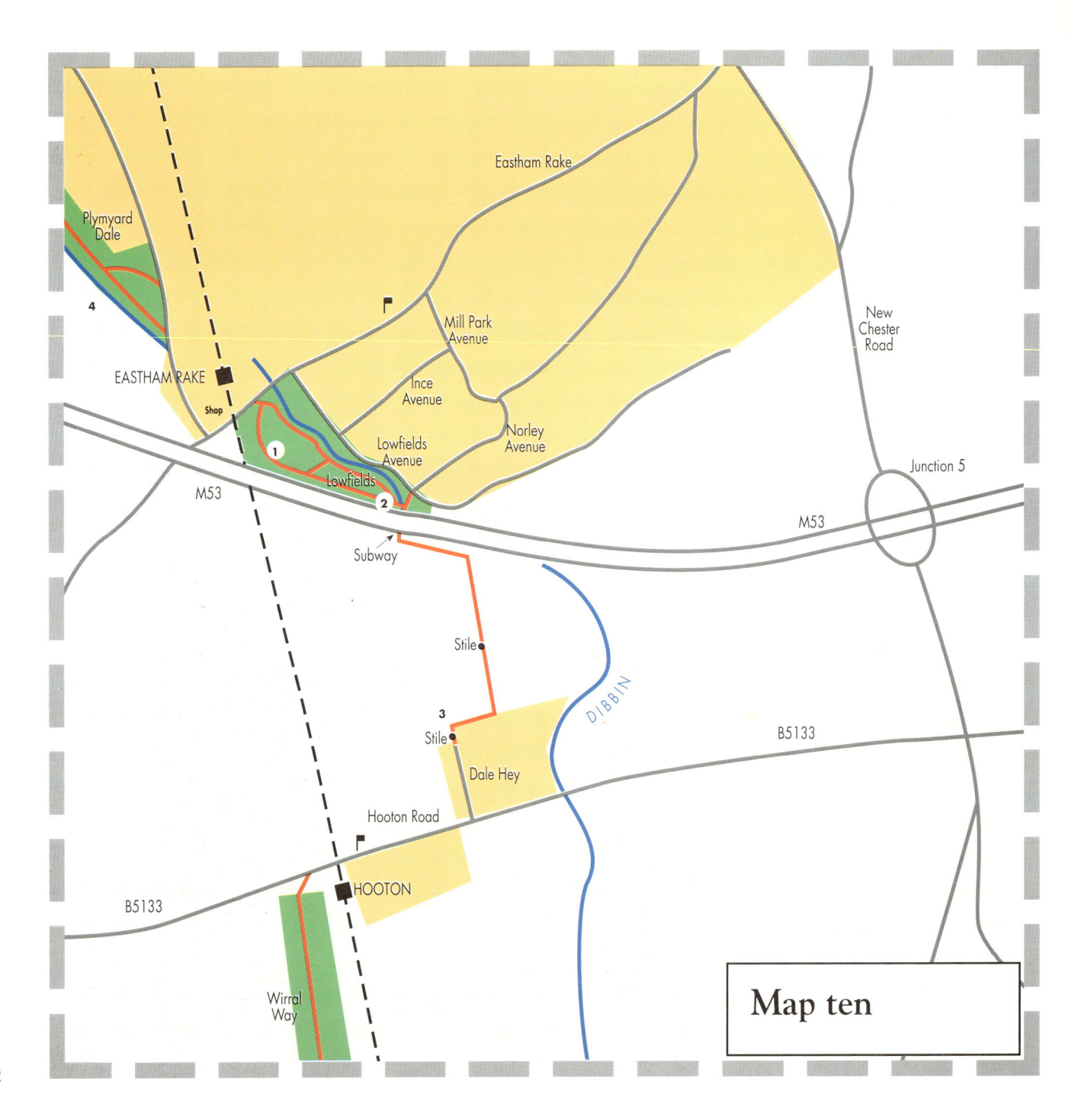

Map ten – While the area focused on in this map is predominantly industrial, there are some places where you can escape to a more rural setting. One such place is the Lowfields (1). A mature woodland and newly coppiced hazel wood, where wet-meadow wildflowers and spring flowers are a speciality, particularly bluebells, which thrive in April and May.

The Dibbin passes through here and it can be seen from the footpath, as indicated on the map. However, the path is uneven and only surfaced in part and access to the river is further limited by several steep sections of path down to its banks. The chevrons (2) indicate the route which is more suitable for wheelchair users or pushchairs, although the path is only roughly surfaced and, therefore, some visitors may find it a little difficult to negotiate. (Contact Eastham Rangers, telephone 0151 327 1007)

General access to the Lowfields can be either from Eastham Rake Road or Lowfields Avenue, or on foot via the path leading from Hooton Road (3). This can also be used as a connection to the Wirral Way, a linear park of nearly 12 miles which follows the route of the old Hooton to West Kirby Railway. The path crosses fields and although the land is level and unploughed, it does get muddy in winter.

The Dibbin usually flows all year round. It is a natural watercourse, that is to say it is not engineered. Unfortunately though it is susceptible to typical urban pollution, for example: fly tipping and run off from roads. The rivers reaction in dealing with pollution results in less oxygen being available for aquatic life. This is one of RiVa 2005's biggest concerns.

The Dibbin is culverted beneath the railway line north of the Lowfields but re-emerges at Plymyard Dale. A Site of Biological Interest you can get to the dale from Brookhurst Avenue, where a short section of woodland valley is accessible to the public. (For further information contact Eastham Country Park, telephone 0151 327 1007)

Just off this map, further along the Wirral Way is Hadlow Road Station. It now serves as a museum and Rangers' office, but the station buildings and part of the platform is preserved to look as it was when closed down in the l950s. (Contact the Cheshire Ranger Service at Hadlow Road for more information, telephone 0151 327 5145

A male broad bodied chaser, found around well vegetated ponds and lakes